Irish Country Inns

BOOKS IN KAREN BROWN'S COUNTRY INN SERIES

Austrian Country Inns & Castles

California - Inns & Itineraries

English, Welsh & Scottish Country Inns

European Country Cuisine - Romantic Inns & Recipes

European Country Inns - Best on a Budget

France - Best Bed & Breakfasts

French Country Inns & Chateaux

German Country Inns & Castles

Irish Country Inns

Italian Country Inns & Villas

Portuguese Country Inns & Pousadas

Scandinavian Country Inns & Manors

Spanish Country Inns & Paradors

Swiss Country Inns & Chalets

Irish Country Inns

JUNE BROWN

Illustrated by

BARBARA TAPP

Karen Brown's Country Inn Series

WARNER BOOKS

TRAVEL PRESS editors: Clare Brown, June Brown
Karen Brown, Iris Sandilands

Cover painting and Illustrations: Barbara Tapp
Maps: Keith Cassell

This book is written in cooperation with:
Town and Country - Hillsdale Travel
16 East Third Avenue, San Mateo, California 94401

This Warner Books edition is published by arrangement with
Travel Press, San Mateo, California 94401

Warner Books, Inc., 666 Fifth Avenue, New York, NY 10103
Ⓦ A Warner Communications Company

Printed in the United States of America
First Warner Books Trade Paperback Printing: March 1988
10 9 8 7 6 5 4 3 2 1

LIBRARY OF CONGRESS
Library of Congress Cataloging-in-Publication Data
Brown, Karen.
    Irish Country Inns / Karen Brown.
        p.   cm.
    Includes index.
    ISBN 0-446-38808-4 (pbk.) (U.S.A.) / 0-446-38954-4(pbk.) (Canada)
    1. Hotels, taverns, etc. ·· Ireland ·· Guide-books. 2. Ireland⁻
    ⁻⁻Description and travel ·· 1981 ·· Guide-books.
    I. Title. II. Title: Irish country inns.
    TX910.I7B76 1988
    647 .9441501 ·· dc19   87-26015
                                      CIP

For Pam & Ann

Contents

Foreword

"Irish Country Inns" is written in the sincere belief that where you stay in Ireland is as much a part of your trip as what you see. The fondest memories of a visit to the Emerald Isle are those of its warm-hearted, friendly people. And there can be no better way to meet the people than to stay with them in their homes and experience a slice of Irish life. To keep you on the right track we have linked many of these charming places together with countryside sightseeing to form four particularly interesting driving itineraries. Dublin is Eire's capital, a large dynamic city where the old and the new, the modern and the traditional exist side by side. To give you an overview of Dublin's fair city we have designed a walking tour that blends culture, history, shopping and that most traditional of Irish drinks, Guinness. In the title the term "inns" is used to mean places to stay that we recommend, establishments that are our favorites, preferably owned and run by a welcoming family. In some cases service may not be the most efficient and occasionally the owners have their eccentricities, which all add to the allure of these small places. Our accommodation section includes 26 farmhouses, 11 guesthouses, 7 country homes, 2 restaurants with rooms, 3 city hotels, 8 traditional inns, 2 castle hotels and 29 country house hotels. There are enough recommendations in every price category to enable you to tailor your trip to your budget. Room rates are quoted in Irish punts (see Rates page 6). We have recommended accommodation in the widest of ranges so please do not expect the same standard of luxury at, for example Greenhill House near Coleraine as at the luxurious Ashford Castle in Cong - there is no comparison - yet each is outstanding in what it offers. Please write to us - your comments and suggestions are invaluable: thanks to your response and through your letters of critique we are able to improve each new edition.

Introduction

Writers wax lyrical about the spectacular scenery, ever-changing landscapes, splendid seascapes, purple moorlands, monastic ruins, enchanting lakes, towering fortresses and winding narrow roads where vast patchworks of fields are spread in every shade of green - believe every word they say.   But, realize that it's the people that make a visit to Ireland special - their open friendliness and warmth of welcome.   And that's what staying in a country inn is all about - experiencing Irish warmth and hospitality.   Ireland is not conducive to rushing: the country roads lend themselves to exploration at a leisurely pace where you return the smile and wave of greeting of those you pass, have time to stop at a pub and be drawn into conversation and, when you get lost, ask directions and learn a bit of history or folklore, as a bonus, along with the directions, leading you to ask again a mile down the road.

CLIMATE

It has been said that there is no such thing as climate in Ireland - only weather. This is because the changes in conditions from day to day and even from hour to hour seem greater than the changes from one season to the next. The Atlantic Ocean and the air masses moving east give Ireland very little seasonal variation in temperature: mild winters and cool summers. The ocean's influence is strongest near the coast, especially in winter when areas bordering the sea are milder than those inland. Coastal areas, particularly in the west, also have less variation in temperature between day and night. Even when it rains, and it does, it never pours - it's just soft Irish rain which keeps the isle emerald. The best thing is to be prepared for sun and sudden squalls at all times.

CLOTHING

Ireland is an easygoing place and casual clothes are acceptable everywhere - even at the fanciest restaurants. Because the weather is changeable layers of sweaters and shirts that can be added to and removed are recommended. A lightweight, waterproof jacket with a hood is indispensable.

CREDIT CARDS

Many places do not accept plastic payment. Whether accommodation accepts payment by credit card is indicated in the accommodation description section using the terms: none, AX - American Express, DC - Diners Club, MC - Master Card and Access, VS - Visa, or simply, all major.

DRIVING

It is to the countryside that you must go, for to visit Ireland without driving through the country areas is to miss the best that she has to offer. Driving is on the left-hand side of the road which may take a little getting used to, so avoid driving in cities until you feel comfortable with the system. If your arrival city is Dublin do not pick your car up until you are ready to leave for the countryside. Your car will not be an automatic unless you specifically reserve one. A valid driver's license is required. Car hire is expensive, so shop around before securing a reservation. Petrol (gasoline) is extremely expensive, so be sure to budget this into the cost of your holiday.

There are very few dual carriageways/divided highways in the Republic of Ireland. Major roads are designated "N" for "national" roads and are the straightest and most direct routes you can take. Minor roads are designated "R" for "regional" roads: their numbers appear rarely, if ever, on signposts and they are usually wide enough for two cars or one tractor. Off the major routes, road signs are not posted as often as you might wish, so when you drive it's best to plan some extra time for asking the way. Asking the way does have its advantages - you get to experience Irish directions from natives always ready to assure you that you cannot miss your destination - which gives you the opportunity of asking another friendly local the way when you do. One of the jo, s of meandering along sparsely travelled country roads is rounding a bend to find that cows (and donkeys) take precedence over cars as they saunter up the middle of the road. When you meet someone on a country road, do return their salute.

The roads through Northern Ireland are excellent, and the signposting is identical to that in England.

ELECTRICITY

The voltage is 240. Most hotels, guesthouses and farmhouses have American-style razor points for 110 volts. If you want to take your favorite hairdryer, make certain it has dual voltage and purchase a kit of various sized and shaped electrical plugs.

FOOD

Ireland has a bountiful harvest of natural products - salmon, trout, lobsters, oysters, prawns, scallops, beef, lamb and pork. Rich yellow butter and thick cream abound - it seems that the Irish have no concept of cholesterol. Meals are not inexpensive. Wholesome and delicious dinners are usually offered by farmhouses and guesthouses but you must make reservations before noon on the day of your arrival. Country houses and hotels offer more elaborate fare of an exceedingly high standard and most have interesting wines. Yet it is the simplest of dishes whose memory remains most vivid: brown soda bread, Irish bacon and sausage, scones, grilled trout fresh from the stream and warm apple pie served piled high with thick yellow cream.

INFORMATION

Before you leave home the Irish Tourist Board can supply you with information on all areas of the Republic and, at your request, specific information on accommodation in homes, farmhouses and manors as well as information on festivals, fishing and the like.

In Ireland the Tourist Offices, known as Bord Failte, have specific information on their area and will, for a small fee, make lodging reservations for you.

ITINERARIES

To keep you on the right track we have formed driving itineraries linking the most interesting sightseeing. Each itinerary is unique in exploiting a particular region's scenic beauty, history and culture. In all but one instance we include choices from different types of accommodations, enabling you to travel from country house hotel to country house hotel or farmhouse to farmhouse. Under each destination our personal recommendation for places to stay is outlined under the title RECOMMENDED LODGING. More detailed descriptions are given in the section "Places to Stay". The amount of sightseeing at a particular destination is an indication of how many days you should spend in a particular area. The capricious changes in the weather mean that often what appears sparkling and romantic in sunshine appears dull and depressing under gathering storm clouds. If the weather is stormy find a nice place with good company and enjoy yourself. Once the rain clears there is much to see.

MAPS

The Overview Map (page 166) shows how the itineraries can be linked together. In addition, at the beginning of each itinerary a map shows that itinerary's routing. We have tried to include as much information as possible but you will need a more detailed map to outline your travels. Our preference is for the Michelin map of Ireland where the scale is 6.30 miles to an inch (1/400,000). At the end of the section "Places to Stay" four maps show the location of the towns and villages nearest to the lodgings. All of these places can be found on the Michelin map.

PLACES TO STAY

This book does not cover the many modern hotels in Ireland with their private bathrooms, televisions and direct-dial phones. Rather, it offers a selection of personally recommended lodgings that cover the widest range from a very basic clean room in a simple farmhouse to a sumptuous suite in an elegant castle. In many the decor is less than perfect. We have inspected each and every one and have stayed in a great many - they are the kind of places that we enjoy. We have tried to describe them accurately to paint a picture of what you can expect to find and what there is to do in the surrounding area.

Owners of guesthouses, farmhouses and bed and breakfasts are usually happy to serve an evening meal if you make arrangements before noon on the same day. The listing states what kind of establishment it is: country house, farmhouse, guesthouse, home, restaurant with rooms, castle, city hotel or traditional inn. The majority of our recommendations are establishments with just a few rooms: staying in these small places you feel as though you are members of the family, sharing homes and sampling facets of Irish life.

RATES are those quoted to us either verbally or by correspondence for the 1988 summer season. The rates given are for the LEAST expensive single room and the MOST expensive double room inclusive of breakfast, all service charges and taxes. Some hotels have two-room suites at higher prices. OR whenever it is appropriate we quote the cost of bed and breakfast per person per night. Please ALWAYS CHECK prices and terms when making a reservation. Rates are quoted in Irish punts.

RESERVATIONS should always be made in advance for Dublin accommodation. In the countryside space is easier and a nice room can often be had simply by calling in the morning. July and August are the busiest times and if you are travelling to a popular spot such as Killarney you should make advance reservations. For those of you who enjoy the security of knowing where you are going to lay your head each night, we suggest that you make advance reservations either directly by phone, by letter if time permits or, in the case of hotels that have one, through the United States representative.

PUBS

Ireland's pubs will not disappoint - if you do not expect sophisticated establishments. Most of the 12,000 pubs where the Irish share ideas over frothing pints of porter have a contagious spirit and charm. Stop at a pub and you'll soon be drawn into conversation. At local pubs musicians and dancers perform for their own enjoyment, their audience being those who stop by for a drink.

ROOTS

The Potato Famine of the 1840s cut population by a fourth. Through the lean decades that followed, the Irish left by the thousands to make new lives primarily in the United States, Canada, Australia and New Zealand. The first step in tracing your Irish roots is to collect together as much information on your Irish antecedents as possible and to find out from relatives or documents (death or marriage certificates) just where he or she came from in Ireland. Armed with this information your choices are several:

Do it yourself: If your ancestors hailed from Southern Ireland visit the genealogical offices on Kildare Street in Dublin. If your ancestors came from Northern Ireland the Public Record Office of Northern Ireland, 66 Balmoral Avenue, Belfast BT9 6YN will be able to assist you.

Have someone do it for you: The genealogical office charges a small fee but due to a huge backlog often takes more than a year to do a general search. Write to Chief Herald, General Office of Ireland, Kildare Street, Dublin 2 enclosing your findings.

A reputable genealogical service such as Hibernian Researchers, 22 Windsor Road, Dublin 6 charges higher fees, moves faster and produces a more comprehensive report. Write to them for details.

If your ancestors came from Northern Ireland send your findings, along with a letter, to one of the following: Ulster Historical Foundation, 66 Balmoral Avenue, Belfast 629 6NY; General Register Office, Oxford House, 49-55 Chichester Street, Belfast BT1 4HL; Presbyterian Historical Society, Church House, Fisherwick Place, Belfast BT1 6DU.

The Irish Tourist Board information sheet number 8, "Tracing Your Ancestors", gives more detailed information and provides information on publications that may be of interest to those of Irish descent.

SHOPPING

Prices of goods are fairly standard throughout Ireland, so make your purchases as you find items you like as it is doubtful that you will find them again at a less expensive price. The most popular items to buy are hand knit sweaters, tweeds, crystal, china and hand embroidered linens.

Value Added Tax (VAT) is included in the price of your purchases. There is usually a minimum purchase requirement, but it is possible for visitors to get a refund of the VAT on the goods they buy in one of two ways:-

1. If the goods are shipped overseas direct from the point of purchase, the store can deduct the VAT at the time of sale.

2. For visitors taking the goods with them ask the store to issue a VAT refund receipt. A passport is needed for identification.   On departure, BEFORE you

check in for your flight, go to the Customs Office at Shannon or Dublin Airport. Your receipts will be stamped and the officer may ask to see your purchases. Check in for your flight and proceed to the VAT refund desk in the departures hall where you will be given a cash refund in the currency of your choice.

An Irish Blessing

May the road rise to meet you,
May the wind be always at your back,
May the sun shine warm upon your face,
May the rains fall soft upon your fields,
And, until we meet again,
May God hold you in the palm of his hand.

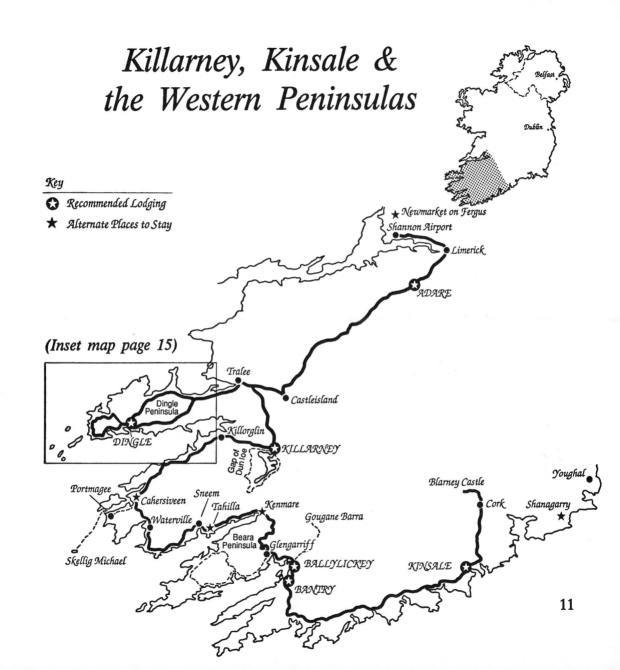

Killarney, Kinsale & the Western Peninsulas

Key

⭐ Recommended Lodging

★ Alternate Places to Stay

Belfast

Dublin

★ Newmarket on Fergus

Shannon Airport

Limerick

ADARE

(Inset map page 15)

Tralee

Dingle Peninsula

Castleisland

Killorglin

DINGLE

Gap of Dunloe

KILLARNEY

Portmagee

Cahersiveen

Sneem

Tahilla

Kenmare

Blarney Castle

Youghal

Waterville

Gougane Barra

Cork

Shanagarry

Skellig Michael

Beara Peninsula

Glengarriff

BALLYLICKEY

KINSALE

BANTRY

11

Killarney, Kinsale & the Western Peninsulas

The scenery of the southwest is absolutely magnificent: the translucent Lakes of Killarney, the ever-changing light on spectacular seascapes on the Dingle Peninsula, the rugged gorges that wind you towards Glengarriff and its island filled with subtropical vegetation and the mellow charm of Kinsale Harbour will delight you. Relish the fabled beauties of this lovely part of Ireland and take part in the tradition of climbing atop Blarney Castle to kiss the stone that is said to confer "the gift of the gab". Do not hurry, allow time to linger over a hearty Irish breakfast, enjoy a chat over a glass of Guinness, sample freshly caught salmon and scallops and join in an evening singsong in a local pub.

Kinsale Harbour

ORIGINATING CITY   LIMERICK-SHANNON AIRPORT

This itinerary begins at SHANNON AIRPORT simply because it is the arrival point of so many overseas visitors. In the main arrivals lounge are a bank, tourist information office and car rental pickup booths. The Shannon Duty-Free Shop is open to departing visitors. It is no longer the bargain it was in days gone by but it certainly proves useful to those who have not had a chance to shop during their stay in Ireland.

DESTINATION I   ADARE

When you leave Shannon Airport follow the N19 south to Limerick. Your destination for tonight, Adare, is just an hour's drive from Shannon and, if you arrive early enough, you can consider sightseeing at BUNRATTY CASTLE AND FOLK PARK which lies just a few miles south of the airport. An interesting history and guide to the castle is available at the entrance. As the majority of castles in Ireland stand roofless and in ruins it is a treat to visit a 15th-century castle that has been restored so beautifully. The authentic 14th- to 17th- century furniture in the rooms is genuine and gives the castle a real lived-in feel. In the evenings firelit banquets warmed with goblets of mead whisk visitors back to the days when the castle was young.

In the castle grounds a folk park contains several cottages, farmhouses and a whole village street of shops, houses and buildings furnished appropriately for their era. The community is brought to life by costumed townspeople who cook, make candles, thatch and farm. BUNRATTY COTTAGE, opposite the castle, offers a wide range of handmade Irish goods and just at the entrance to the park is DURTY NELLY'S, one of Ireland's most popular pubs, dating from the 1600s.

The city of LIMERICK is a busy metropolis whose traffic-crowded streets have to be negotiated with a degree of caution. Leave Limerick on the N20 leading to the N21 and it is only a half-hour drive to your destination ADARE with its charming row of thatched cottages, its tree-lined streets and interesting old churches making it one of the most picturesque villages in Ireland.

RECOMMENDED LODGING

The DUNRAVEN ARMS has welcomed guests for more than 160 years. What was originally a coaching inn now offers the flavor and feel of a country house with nicely decorated bedrooms, a snug lounge, a sumptuous dining room and the discreet service of uniformed staff. If less formal dining is to your taste, the hotel has a most charming thatched cottage restaurant across the street.

If you are travelling the bed and breakfast way you can do no better than to stay with Mary Dundon at ABBEY VILLA. The house is a modern bungalow on an urban street just off the main road. All the bedrooms are prettily decorated and have private bathrooms. While this modern bungalow does not have a country-cozy warmth that you find in older establishments, you are ensured of a good night's rest and a central location for exploring the town.

Today the DINGLE PENINSULA beckons. It's a very special place, a narrow promontory of harshly beautiful land and seascapes where the people are especially friendly and welcoming to strangers. The road from Adare to Dingle town takes you southwest on the N21 through CASTLEISLAND and TRALEE where you leave the main road and continue on to the peninsula through DERRYMORE. At CAMP the road divides and both roads lead to Dingle. Choose the coast route through STRANDBALLY and BALLYDUFF, for it brings you to the CONNOR PASS road which twists you upwards to the summit where Dingle and its sheltered harbour come into sight far below. The view is one of the most entrancing things about this peninsula but there is no guarantee that you will see it. All will be green fields and sparkling blue sea and sky, until the mists roll in and everything vanishes. Conversely, you are driving along in mist and squall when suddenly the clouds part, the sun pours down and the most beautiful vistas appear. Narrow roads lead into the shop- and pub-lined main street of DINGLE town, the largest settlement on the peninsula. The occasional windowbox brightens the plain gray houses and fishing boats bob in the harbour unloading bountiful catches of fish and shellfish. It is not surprising that you find a great many excellent seafood restaurants here.

The Dingle Peninsula

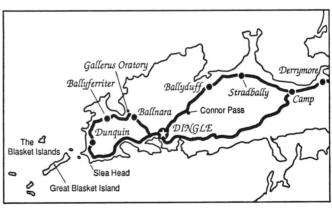

RECOMMENDED LODGING:

DOYLE'S SEAFOOD BAR AND TOWN-HOUSE offers accommodation and fine dining in the heart of the town. Slate floors, brick walls, pine tables and sugan (wood and rope) chairs add an old-fashioned charm to the restaurant set in what was once a small village shop and pub. The house next door has been extended to the rear to provide eight bedrooms, each with private bathroom, and decorated to match the style of the old building.

A little over a mile out of town, on the road to Slea Head, CLEEVAUN has the advantage of being purposely built as a bed and breakfast. All the bedrooms have private bathrooms and are prettily decorated with sprigged papers, matching curtains and bedspreads and pine furniture. The Sheehys offer a wealth of both verbal and written information on the sights, ruins, traditions and folklore of the peninsula. Watching the ever-changing interplay of sunlight and mist on the bay turns breakfast into a lingering meal.

Check in at your accommodation and reserve this afternoon for exploration of the beautiful beaches and rocky promontories that lie to the west of Dingle town. The road to SLEA HEAD twists and turns, following the contours of the increasingly rocky coast, stunning seascapes present themselves demanding that you pause just to admire the view.

As you round Slea Head the BLASKET ISLANDS come into view - alternately sparkling like jewels in the blue ocean and disappearing under dark and gathering clouds a moment later. The islands have been uninhabited since 1953 when the last islanders evacuated their windswept abode.

A small boat ferries daytrip visitors to and from GREAT BLASKET ISLAND. It leaves daily (May to September) from Dunquin Harbour at 11.00am returning in the late afternoon. As the boat leaves only in clear, calm weather call 56280 before setting out. The little village on the island is mostly in ruins and paths wander amongst the fields where the hardy islanders struggled to earn a living.

DUNQUIN'S pier sits away from the scattered village and is reached by a steep path that zigzags down the cliff. As you round the last twist you see curraghs turned upside down looking like giant black beetles stranded high above the water line . Curraghs are fragile boats made of tarred canvas stretched over a wooden skeleton. Saint Brendan is reputed to have discovered America in such a boat.

Over a thousand years ago many of Saint Brendan's contemporaries lived on the Dingle Peninsula in unmortared beehive-shaped stone huts called clochans. You will see many such huts on the peninsula and the most famous example is the GALLERUS ORATORY, a tiny church built not as a circle but in the shape of an upturned boat. It has a small window at one end, a small door at the other and is as watertight today as when it was built over 900 years ago. (The oratory is located beyond BALLYFERRITER.) From here the road takes you south to BALLNARA, MILLTOWN and back to Dingle.

Plan to spend at least two nights on the peninsula to take the trip to the Blasket Islands and to afford time to wander along the beaches or walk along the hedgerow-lined lanes dividing the fields where friendly locals pause from their work to call a greeting and wave a salute of welcome.

DESTINATION III   KILLARNEY

Leaving the Dingle Peninsula return to Tralee and take the N22 for the 21-mile drive to KILLARNEY. Believe everything you ever read about the magnificent beauty of the Killarney lakes but realize that the town is absolutely packed with tourists during the summer season. But, do not despair: your lodgings lie beyond the busy throng.

RECOMMENDED LODGING:

CAHERNANE HOTEL was once a grand country home rescued from decline to be restored and refurbished as a lovely country house hotel. Bedrooms in the original house have lots of charm while those in the new adjoining wing have stylish modern decor.

CARRIGLEA HOUSE commands a captivating view of the Lower Lake and its backdrop of mountains. Marie and Michael Beazley's 200-year-old home is extremely popular with visitors and reservations should be made in advance. Several of the bedrooms enjoy private bathrooms - bedrooms in the converted coach house are the most attractive.

KATHLEEN'S COUNTRY HOUSE offers accommodation in a modern guesthouse. Kathleen takes especially good care of her visitors, always finding time for a friendly chat and cooking very nice breakfasts and dinners. The bedrooms are freshly decorated and fitted out with good firm beds, televisions, tea-making facilities and private bathrooms.

After settling into your lodgings, spend the afternoon at MUCKROSS HOUSE and GARDENS 3 miles out of Killarney on the Kenmare road. Leave your car outside the lower entrance to the estate and hire a jaunting car to take you through the grounds alongside the lake to the house and gardens, or, if you prefer, you can take one of the lovely walks that bring you to the house. (A second entrance, farther down the Kenmare road, gives access to a car park adjacent to the house.) Muckross House was built in 1843 in a Tudor style. Much of the interior is furnished in a Victorian manner and the remainder of the house serves as a folk museum with various exhibits. There is also a blacksmith, potter, gift shop and tearoom. The gardens surrounding the house contain many subtropical plants.

Farther along the Kenmare road you come to the car park for TORC WATERFALL. Following the stream, a short uphill walk brings you to the celebrated 60-foot cascade of water.

If you are in the mood for an evening adventure (this is not a trip that should be attempted on a wet rainsoaked evening) you can drive through the beautiful GAP OF DUNLOE and emerge back on the road to Killarney just west of Moll's Gap. If you decide to drive you must leave it until after seven in the evening as the daytime horse traffic on this narrow unpaved road will not let you pass! Leave Killarney on the Killorglin road and after passing the golf course make a left-hand turn at the signpost for the Gap of Dunloe.

KATE KEARNEY'S COTTAGE is at the entrance to the ravine. Legend has it that Kate was a beautiful witch who drove men wild with desire. Now her home is greatly enlarged as a coffee and souvenir shop. Beyond the cottage the road continues as a single-lane dirt track up a 4-mile ravine carved by glaciers. The dramatic setting is enhanced by the Purple Mountains on your left and Macgillicuddy's Reeks on your right. As you drive up the gorge the sides rise ever steeper and pass deep glacial lakes - the farther you travel into the gap the more you are moved by its haunting beauty. Cresting the ravine the track winds down into another valley and becomes a single-lane paved road with passing places that joins the N71 to the west of the narrow passage through the rocks known as MOLL'S GAP. Following the road back into town, you come to LADIES' VIEW which on a clear evening offers unparalleled views of the Lakes of Killarney. From here you return to Killarney.

If you would like additional views of the lakes, then a tour to Aghadoe Hill or a boat trip from Ross Castle should give you what you are looking for. Leave Killarney on the road to Tralee (N22) and turn left for the 3-mile drive to AGHADOE where Killarney town, lakes and mountains can all be seen from this vantage point. If you prefer a close look at the lake and its islands, 90-minute boat tours of the Lower Lake leave from the jetty alongside the ruin of Ross Castle. Tickets for this trip should be purchased from the Tourist Office in town.

SIDETRIP TO SKELLIG MICHAEL

SKELLIG MICHAEL is a very special place, a rocky island topped by the ruins of an ancient monastery lying 10 miles off the coast of the Ring of Kerry. Arriving at the cove beneath the looming rock, the first part of your ascent follows the path to the abandoned lighthouse past puffins' nests clinging to tiny crevasses in the steep rock slopes. Rounding a corner, the monks' stairway appears and it's up hundreds and hundreds of hand hewn stone steps to the monastery perched on a ledge high above the pounding ocean. Pausing to catch your breath, you wonder at the monks who set out in fragile little boats to establish this monastery and toiled with crude implements to build these steps up the sheer rock face.

At the summit six little beehive huts, a slightly larger stone oratory and the roofless walls of a small church nestle against the hillside, some poised at the edge - only a low stone wall between them and the churning ocean far below. The windowless interiors of the huts hardly seem large enough for a man to lie down. Remarkably, the monks' only water source was rainwater runoff stored in rock fissures.

It is not known when the monks arrived. According to annals, the Vikings raided in 812 and 823 and found an established community and it is documented that the last monks departed in the 13th century. When it is time to leave this spot there is a sense of wonder at the men who toiled in this rocky place, enduring deprivation, hardship and solitude to achieve a state of grace.

The park service is maintaining and restoring the site and there may be someone to impart information.

No boats are government-licensed to make the trip to Skellig Michael, but I was very comfortable with the arrangements I made with Des Lavelle, tel: 0667 6124. Des has served with the local lifeboat, written an authoritative book on Skellig Michael and operates a scuba diving school. His boat leaves from Valencia Island stopping to pick up passengers at Portmagee. Remember to wear flat heeled shoes and take a waterproof jacket, an extra sweater and lunch.

The trip to Skellig Michael cannot be counted upon till the actual day because it depends on the seas being calm. The morning departure for the island and the late afternoon return necessitates your spending two additional nights on the Ring of Kerry, with TAHILLA COVE GUESTHOUSE at TAHILLA COVE and MOUNT RIVERS at CAHERSIVEEN as lodging recommendations.

Leave Killarney for KILLORGLIN to begin your drive around the RING OF KERRY and hope that the fickle Irish weather is at its best, for when mists wreathe the ring it takes a lot of imagination to conjure up seascapes as you drive down fog-shrouded lanes.   Even if the weather is dull do not lose heart - at any moment the sun could break through.

Beginning the Ring, a pleasant drive takes you across wild moorlands to CAHERSIVEEN.   The most beautiful coastal scenery on this largest of the three westerly peninsulas lies between WATERVILLE and SNEEM.   Sneem is the most picturesque village on the Ring, with its tiny gaily painted houses bordering two village greens.   Concluding the Ring, the road borders the Kenmare River estuary to bring you to KENMARE.   This pleasant town of gray stone houses lining two broad main streets is a summer favorite with tourists who prefer its peace and charm to the hectic pace of Killarney.

From Kenmare, the road to Glengarriff wends upwards.   As it climbs, green fields give way to sparse rocky hillsides.   At the summit the road tunnels through a large buttress of rock and you emerge to a stunning view of BANTRY BAY lying beyond a patchwork of green fields.

As you drive through GLENGARRIFF various boatmen will hail you to select their boat for a 10-minute ride to Garinish Island.   Do not be put off by their good natured banter, for it is a most worthwhile trip.

GARINISH ISLAND, once a barren rock where only gorse and heather grew, was transformed into a miniature botanical paradise at the beginning of this century by a Scots politician, Arran Bryce.   The sheltered site of the island provides perfect growing conditions for trees, shrubs and flowers from all over the world.   It took a hundred men over three years to sculpture this lovely spot with its formal Italian garden, caseta and temple.

RECOMMENDED LODGING:

At *BALLYLICKEY, SEA VIEW HOUSE HOTEL is a gaunt, bright white structure offering far more country-cozy appeal inside than the stark white exterior suggests. Kathleen O'Sullivan offers an especially warm welcome and wonderful food. Rooms at the front of the house offer stunning views through the trees to Bantry Bay.*

A few miles farther along the coastal road, just beyond BANTRY, on the left-hand side of the road, is the entrance to BANTRY HOUSE, a grand mansion dating from 1750, commanding the loveliest of views over Bantry Bay. Fortunately for visitors, one wing of the house has been rescued from ruin and renovated to provide bed and breakfast accommodation. The rooms are very attractive in their decor. Further renovation is under way and until building is completed guests take their meals around a pine table in the old kitchen which doubles as a tea-room for daytime visitors to the house.

The main portion of Bantry House is still occupied by the descendants of the Earls of Bantry who open up its huge, grand rooms to the public. Guide sheets tour you through the opulent rooms filled with elegant European furniture, tapestries and paintings. Portraits of the ancestors of the Earls of Bantry gaze down upon you: by contrast to his demure forebears the current occupant, Egerton Shellswell-White, is portrayed playing his trombone.

A second night in this lovely corner of Ireland gives you the time to wander off the main roads and explore the BEARA PENINSULA with its stunning views of barren rocky mountains, wild, tumbling streams and rocky bays set against a slate-gray sea. Return to Glengarriff and turn left in the centre of the town towards CASTLETOWNBERE, following the narrow road that hugs the ocean. At the first T junction turn right and begin the 4-mile ascent up the HEALY PASS. It's hard to turn and admire the views of BANTRY BAY as the road gently zigzags to the top of the pass, so pause at the top and look back, but do not stay too long as the most spectacular view of GLANMORE LAKE and the Kenmare River Bay awaits you as you gently wend your way downwards. (This trip should not be undertaken on any but the clearest of days.) Turn left at LAURAGH and make your way around the peninsula back to Glengarriff.

The trip around the Beara Peninsula takes about 2 1/2 hours, leaving the afternoon free for an inland excursion to GOUGANE BARRA, a beautiful lake locked into a ring of mountains. Here you find a small hotel for a snack or a warming drink, and a little church on an island in the lake, the oratory where Saint Finbarr went to contemplate and pray. The road to and from the lake takes you over a high pass and through mountain tunnels.

DESTINATION V   KINSALE

Leave the shores of Bantry Bay to the south, following the N71. As the road turns eastward the barren rocky countryside gradually gives way to verdant, rolling fields in every shade of green. Pass through SKIBBEREEN and on through CLONAKILTY. Shortly after leaving the town turn right, following country lanes to TIMOLEAGUE, a small coastal village watched over by the ruins of a Franciscan abbey. After tracing the coast for 6 miles, turn inland for the 4-mile drive to BALLINSPITTLE. Driving through this sleepy little village, it is hard to imagine that in 1985 it was overwhelmed by pilgrims. They came to the village shrine after a local girl reported seeing the statue of the Virgin Mary rocking back and forth. You pass the shrine as you take the road to Kinsale.

Across the Bandon River and round the headland, KINSALE comes into view, its harbour full of tall-masted boats. Narrow winding streets lined both with quaint and several sadly derelict houses lead up from the harbour. Flowers abound: small posies tucked into little baskets, spilling from windowboxes and artistically planted at every turn - small wonder that Kinsale won the "Tidy Towns" competition in 1986.

There has been a fortress here since Norman times. A great battle nearby in 1601 precipitated the flight of the earls and sounded the death knell of the ancient Gaelic civilization. It was from Kinsale that James II left for exile after his defeat at Boyne Water. Bypassed by 20th-century events, Kinsale has emerged as a village full of character, attracting visitors who find themselves seduced by its charms.

About 2 miles east of Kinsale the impressive 17th-century CHARLES FORT stands guard over the entrance to its harbour. It takes several hours to tour the five bastions that make up the complex. The ordnance sheds are restored and hold a photographic and historical exhibition about the fort.

Across the esturary you see the 1603 JAMES FORT where William Penn's father was governor of Kinsale, while William worked as a clerk of the Admiralty Court. Later William was given a land grant in America on which he founded the state of Pennsylvania.

RECOMMENDED LODGING

The *BLUE HAVEN HOTEL* has a reputation for its fine seafood restaurant. In 1981 Bloomingdales of New York invited its owners, Brian and Anne Cronin, to present a range of their special seafood dishes in its restaurant. A friendly pub and sheltered flower-filled patio offer alternative places for less formal dining. Upstairs the bedrooms are delightfully decorated and reflect the care and attention that Brian and Anne have lavished on every aspect of their charming little hotel.

Sitting high on the hill overlooking the harbour, *ARDCARRIG* is home to Bill and Bobbe Gilmore who emigrated to Ireland from America. They run their lovely antique-filled home as an informal country house.

THE LIGHTHOUSE is the most delightful bed and breakfast in Kinsale. Ruthann and Art, who also hail from America, love to welcome visitors to their cozy home where every nook and cranny is filled with country bygones. The tiny bedrooms are beautifully decorated and a feeling of warmth and welcome pervades this comfortable home.

Your travel options at the conclusion of this itinerary are many: you can continue north to Limerick to follow THE BURREN, CONNEMARA & ACHILL ISLAND itinerary, return to Shannon Airport, or continue west joining THE WICKLOW MOUNTAINS, WATERFORD, CASHEL & KILKENNY itinerary in Youghal and reversing it as it traverses along the coast through Waterford and the Wicklow Mountains to Dublin.

Whichever route you decide to follow, you are only a short drive from BLARNEY CASTLE and its famous tourist attraction, the BLARNEY STONE. Kissing the Blarney Stone, by climbing atop the keep and hanging upside down 80 feet in the air, is said to confer the "gift of the gab".

Blarney Castle

The Burren, Connemara & Achill Island

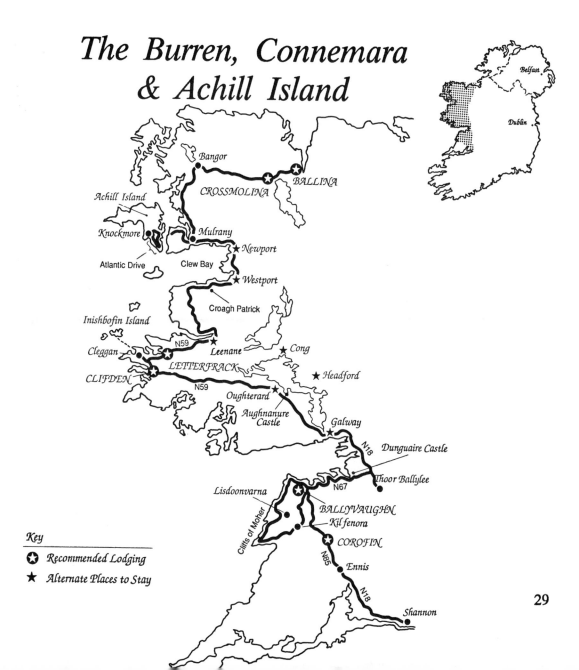

Belfast

Dublin

Bangor

CROSSMOLINA

BALLINA

Achill Island

Knockmore

Mulrany

Newport

Atlantic Drive

Clew Bay

Westport

Croagh Patrick

Inishbofin Island

N59

Leenane

Cong

Cleggan

LETTERFRACK

Headford

CLIFDEN

N59

Oughterard

Aughnanure Castle

Galway

Dunguaire Castle

N18

Lisdoonvarna

N67

Thoor Ballylee

BALLYVAUGHN

Cliffs of Moher

Kilfenora

COROFIN

N85

Ennis

N18

Shannon

Key

⭐ Recommended Lodging

★ Alternate Places to Stay

29

The Burren, Connemara & Achill Island

This itinerary takes you off the beaten tourist track through the wild, hauntingly beautiful scenery of County Clare, Connemara and County Mayo. Lying on the coast of County Clare, the Burren presents a vast landscape of smooth limestone rocks whose crevices are ablaze with rock roses, blue gentians and all manner of Arctic and Alpine flowers in the spring and early summer. Otherwise there are no trees, shrubs, rivers or lakes - just bare moonscapes of rocks dotted with forts and ruined castles, tombs and rock cairns. Travelling to Connemara, your route traces the vast island-dotted Lough Corrib and traverses boglands and moorlands, the distant mountains fill the horizon and guide you to the coast where gentle waves lap at rocky inlets sheltering scattered villages and whitewashed cottages dot the landscape. Ireland's holy mountain, Croagh Patrick, and the windswept Achill Island leave a deep impression on the visitor. This itinerary winds through some of the most unpopulated areas of Ireland, where often the only person for miles is a lone peat cutter chopping bricks of dark brown turf and stacking them to dry alongside the road.

Clifden

This itinerary begins at SHANNON AIRPORT, a most convenient starting point for a west coast itinerary. Shannon Airport is the destination of planes from all over the world and here passengers begin their "Irish holiday". In the main arrivals lounge are a bank, tourist information office and car rental pickup booths.

DESTINATION I   BALLYVAUGHAN .or COROFIN

Leaving the airport grounds, it is less than an hour's drive to either of the recommended accommodations. If you are not too tired, detour just a few miles to the south to sightsee at BUNRATTY CASTLE AND FOLK PARK (page 13). Leaving the folk park, turn north and follow the N18 north through ENNIS. At the roundabout on the far side of town take the first left (N85 LAHINCH) - travel a short distance along this road and take the first turn to the right to COROFIN.

RECOMMENDED LODGING:

Shortly after leaving Corofin you see FERGUS VIEW farmhouse on your left. The bedrooms are very small and simply decorated but snug central heating ensures that they are always toasty warm. Mary does a very nice job of producing very tasty farmhouse dinners using lots of vegetables fresh from the garden.

If you prefer a superlative country house hotel, then continue on to the Burren bearing right at the ruins of LEAMANEH CASTLE and across rocky countryside, as you crest the hill you see BALLYVAUGHAN and GREGAN'S CASTLE nestled in the valley below. The ground floor suites are exquisite and have their own doors leading to the garden - even the smallest of bedrooms is quite lovely. The food is amongst the very best you will find anywhere in Ireland and the view from the dining room of the distant Galway Bay is stunning on a fine evening.

Reserve today for explorations of this vast lunarscape of rounded hills where Arctic, Mediterranean and Alpine plants flourish in tiny crevices. Ludlow, one of Cromwell's generals, passing through the area in 1649, wrote, "There is not enough wood to hang a man, nor water to drown him, nor earth enough to bury him in."

CORKSCREW HILL rises directly behind Gregan's Castle hotel. The road winds its way upwards and affords a view worth a photo or two as it rounds the last "corkscrew" bend.

As it is on the route it is worth taking a look at CAHERMACNAGHTER, a few scant remains of what was until 1606 a famous Irish law school. The nearby village of KILLFENORA, just off the Burren proper, has an interpretive centre which offers a 15-minute lecture and 10-minute film on the geology and rare flora and fauna of the area. Next to the display centre an old churchyard contains some interesting high crosses with symbolic carvings.

Turn right as you leave the interpretive centre and left as you come to the main road to reach your destination, the CLIFFS OF MOHER, the most spectacular section of the coastline, where towering cliffs rise above the pounding Atlantic Ocean. These majestic cliffs stretching along 5 miles of the coast are one of Ireland's most popular sights. The visitors' centre offers welcome shelter on cool and windy days.

On leaving the cliffs, retrace your steps, heading north towards LISDOONVARNA and follow the coastal road around Black Head where the rocky Burren spills into Galway Bay. As the road begins to turn inland from the sea and fields replace rocky outcrops, watch for a fingerpost signpost on the left indicating that a right turn into a cart track will bring you to NEWTOWN CASTLE. Follow the track for several miles to the castle - interesting because it is a sturdy 16th-century defensive tower set on a broad square base. (The adjacent farm was being restored, as a home, at the time of our visit and hopefully its completion will lead to the area around the castle being tidied up.) The tower is in remarkably good shape, its domed first- and third-story ceilings still intact. As you leave take the lane at the side of the castle for the 200-yard drive to the main road where a right turn will return you to Gregan's Castle hotel. But the day's sightseeing is not over, so turn left at the main road for the Ailwee Caves await your exploration.

Sitting high on a rocky bluff, the AILWEE CAVES Visitors' Centre is so cleverly designed that it is hard to distinguish it from the surrounding gray landscape. Beneath the eerie moonscape of the Burren lie vast caves and streams and lakes and you can take a tour through a small section of these underground caverns. The first cave is called Bear Haven because the bones of a brown bear who died long ago were found here. In other chambers you see limestone cascades, stalactites and stalagmites before the tour ends at the edge of an underground river. Remember to dress warmly for it's cool in the caves.

From the caves, Gregan's Castle is just a few miles across the valley or Fergus View farmhouse lies to your left a short distance across the Burren.

As you leave the Burren head directly for the coast and follow it east (N67) to KINVARA, a pretty village with boats bobbing in the harbour and small rocky islands separating it from the expanse of Galway Bay. On the outskirts of the village, DUNGUAIRE CASTLE has been restored, and a visit here is interesting as a contrast to Newtown Castle. In the evenings the castle is open for medieval banquets.

From the castle car park, turn towards the village and immediately take a left-hand turn (opposite the castle entrance) for the 5-mile drive to ARDRAHAN where you turn right on the N18 and after 4 miles left for the short drive to THOOR BALLYLEE. William Butler Yeats bought this 16th-century tower house in 1916 and used it as his summer home for 13 years. A self-guided tour, with headphones and tape recorders, guides you round his home to the accompaniment of extracts from his poetry.

Leaving Thoor Ballylee, retrace your steps to the N18 for a 15-mile drive to GALWAY. Follow signs for the city centre and once you are there for CLIFDEN (N59). Be warned: keep your eyes peeled to avoid getting totally lost. Leaving the town behind you, the road is straight and well paved but a tad bouncy if you try to go too fast. (If you look at your map you will see a scenic coastal road marked - do not take it. By far the best route is the inland one. The road which meanders along the coast is outlined later in this itinerary.) Accommodation signs for nearby Oughterard alert you to watch for a right-hand turn to AUGHNANURE CASTLE.

Approaching the castle, you may be greeted, as we were, by a friendly family of goats snoozing on the wooden footbridge before the castle gates. Aughnanure Castle was the stronghold of the ferocious O'Flahertys who launched attacks on

Galway town until their castle was destroyed by English forces in 1572. The clan regained their castle for a period of time until wars with Cromwell and William of Orange saw them expelled again. Nearby OUGHTERARD is a lovely town ("the gateway to Connemara") whose main street has several attractive shops.

The road (N59) continues on to CLIFDEN (50 miles) and the Twelve Pins mountains dominate the wild, almost treeless, landscape of bogs and lakes and rivers. Clifden is the major market town of Connemara and the home of the annual Connemara Pony Show.

RECOMMENDED LODGING

ROCK GLEN COUNTRY HOUSE near CLIFDEN is an engaging place, with cozy public rooms occupying what was once a hunting lodge. Bedrooms are in a more modern section of the hotel, uniform in size and plainly decorated with handwoven bedspreads topping the beds. John and Evangeline place the emphasis on traditional country house hospitality and create a very warm, welcoming atmosphere.

When I think of Irish country house hotels, I think of ROSLEAGUE MANOR near LETTERFRACK where the combined efforts of a brother-sister team, Anne and Patrick Foyle, have created a place of great Irish charm. Glowing peat fires, antiques and attractive decor add to the appeal of this old house overlooking Ballynakill Bay.

ROSE COTTAGE (CLIFDEN) offers extremely simple accommodation in a tidy bed and breakfast. At the heart of the building is a very old traditional cottage where guests are served breakfast and dinner.

Bright sunny days invite exploration of the picturesque coastline that slopes gently to the sea. Little boats anchor in rocky inlets and cottages gaze westward across rocky islands. Leave Clifden to the south, passing the marshy area where Alcock and Brown crash-landed after the first transatlantic flight in 1919 (commemorated by a monument about half a mile from the main road), to BALLINABOY, BALLYCONNEELY and ROUNDSTONE. The sweeping seascapes that this route presents are so compelling that it is difficult to concentrate on the driving.

If the weather is fine a delightful daytrip can be taken to INISHBOFIN ISLAND. (Or if you prefer you can overnight on the island at DAY'S HOTEL.) The Inishbofin boat leaves from Cleggan pier at 11.30am returning at 5pm (the crossing takes less than an hour). Be at Cleggan pier half an hour before sailing time and buy your ticket at the Pier Bar. Sailings depend on weather conditions so it's best to phone ahead on (095) 44261 and verify departure times.

The boat sails into the sheltered harbour presided over by the remains of a Cromwellian castle, and you wade ashore at a cluster of houses that make up the island's main settlement. Many islanders have left in search of greener pastures and their cottages have fallen into disrepair, but those who remain eke out a hard living from the land and the sea. As you walk down lanes edged with wild fuschias and brightly colored wildflowers, whitewashed farmhouses appear and the fields are dotted with handmade haystacks. (Regrettably, the odd long-abandonded rusting car spoils the scene.). At the far side of the island a row of cottages fronts the beach, one of them housing a welcoming little restaurant, THE LOBSTER POT, where you can have a lunch or tea before walking back to the harbour to take the evening boat back to Cleggan.

For shopping there is no better place than CONNEMARA HANDCRAFTS, a mile out of Letterfrack on the Clifden road. This is one of the finest craft shops in Ireland offering a splendid array of Irish goods and serving superlative homemade goodies in its tea shop.

DESTINATION III   BALLINA or CROSSMOLINA

Leaving Clifden, the N59 passes the much photographed KYLEMORE ABBEY. Originally built by a wealthy Englishman in the 19th century, this grand home, surrounded by greenery and fronting a lake, passed into the hands of Benedictine nuns who have a school here. Visitors are welcome to visit the pottery in the grounds.

Follow the shore of KILLARY HARBOUR, the longest and certainly the most picturesque fjord in Ireland, to LEENANE, a little village nestled at the head of the inlet. Continue along the shoreline and take the first turn to the left, signposted as a scenic route to Westport via Louisburgh. This interesting side road gently winds you over hilly moorland and through passes to bring you to Croagh Patrick, the most holy of Irish mountains.

The summit of the conical-shaped CROAGH PATRICK, crowned by swirling mists, substantiates its mystical place in Irish history. It was after Saint Patrick spent the 40 days of Lent atop its rocky summit in 441 AD that the mountain became sacred to the Christian God. Every year thousands of penitential pilgrims begin their climb to the oratory at the summit at dawn on the last Sunday in July. Several go barefoot up the stony track.   On a clear day a walk towards the summit affords a panoramic view across Clew Bay to Achill Island.

Nearby WESTPORT lies on the shore of Clew Bay and is unique amongst Irish towns because it was built following a pre-designed plan.   The architect walled the river and lined the riverside malls with lime trees and austere Georgian homes - forming a most delightful thoroughfare.

Superb views of the island-studded Clew Bay are offered on the road from NEWPORT to MULRANY whence it is only 8 miles to the bridge that separates the mainland from ACHILL ISLAND, Ireland's largest offshore island. Traditionally the Achill islanders travelled to Scotland as migrant farmworkers during the summer, but now what population has not been enticed away by emigration remains to garner a meager living from a harsh land.   It was the home of the infamous British Captain Boycott who gave his name to the English language when tenants "boycotted" him for his excessive rents during the potato famine. Today this island holds the allure that belongs to wild and lonely places: in sunshine it is glorious, but in torrential rain it is a grim and depressing place.

On the island take the first turn to your left, signposted for your destination the windswept ATLANTIC DRIVE where you drive along the tops of rugged cliffs carved by the pounding Atlantic Ocean far below. The "drive" ends at KNOCKMORE where scattered houses shelter from the biting winds.   Return to Mulrany and turn north on the N59 for the 40-mile drive across boglands, where vast quantities of turf are harvested by mechanical means, to BANGOR and on to CROSSMOLINA (26 miles).

RECOMMENDED LODGING

ENNISCOE HOUSE near CROSSMOLINA is a lovely Georgian home isolated within a great estate. The house is beautifully furnished and decorated in a classic Georgian style yet it has a real homey feel to it, with family memorabilia, books and magazines and comfortable arrangements of chairs and sofas around the fire. The large bedrooms at the front are particularly lovely.

KILMURRAY HOUSE lies several miles to the south of Enniscoe House. Madge Moffat was raised in London and when she came here she decided to take guests into her farmhouse. Her husband Joe is is extremely interested in fishing and happy to make arrangements for guests. Several of the tidy bedrooms have private bathrooms.

Activities at **MOUNT FALCON**, near **BALLINA**, centre around the pursuit of fish. While guests go their separate ways during the day, they gather in the evening and dine together with the owner Constance Aldridge presiding at head of table - fishy talk predominates. Bedrooms are decidedly old-fashioned and rather lacking in appealing decor, but the drawing room offers a warmth of welcome with its blazing fire and comfortable arrangement of sofas and chairs.

Your travel options at the conclusion of this itinerary include continuing north to Sligo to follow the YEATS COUNTRY, COUNTY DONEGAL & THE GIANT'S CAUSEWAY itinerary or returning south. As you travel south consider visiting either BALLINTUBBER ABBEY, a beautifully restored church that dates back to 1216, or the village of KNOCK. A religious apparition seen on the gable of the village church in 1879 and some hearty promotion has led to the development of Knock as a religious pilgrimage site and a tourist venue. A giant basilica stands next to the little church, a large complex of religious souvenir shops is across the road and nearby Knock Airport has a runway capable of providing landing facilities for large jets. Surrounded as it is by narrow country lanes this sophisticated complex seems very out of place in rural Ireland.

Belfast

Dublin

RATHMULLEN

RAMELTON

Tamney

Dunfanaghy

Giant's Causeway

Dunluce Castle

Carrick-a-Rede Rope Bridge

Torr Head

Gweedore (Gaoth Dobhair)

N56

N56

N13

COLERAINE

Bushmills

A2

Cushendun

Annagary

Glenveagh Park

Letterkenny

A2

A37

Limavady

A26

Cushendall

Dunglow (An Globhan Liath)

Derry

Glenariff Forest Park

Carnlough

Glencolumbkille Folk Museum

Maas

Ardara

BRUCKLESS

Kilcar

Donegal

N15

Ballymena

A36

Larne

Ulster American Folk Park

Omagh

Grange

Lough Erne

Belleek Pottery

A46

Drumcliff Churchyard

N16

Enniskillen

Sligo

DROMAHAIR

RIVERSTOWN

Marble Arch Caves

Key

Recommended Lodging

Alternate Places to Stay

Border

Yeats Country, County Donegal
& the Giant's Causeway

The northernmost reaches of Ireland hold special appeal. Herein lies the countryside that inspired the moving poetry of William Butler Yeats. Beyond Donegal narrow roads twist and turn around the wild rugged coastline of County Donegal where villagers weave their tweeds and Irish is often the spoken language and that written on the signposts. The Folk Village Museum at Glencolumbkille, with its authentically furnished thatch topped cottages, demonstrates the harsh living conditions of the far north. Crossing into Northern Ireland, the honeycomb columns of the Giant's Causeway signpost the Antrim coast full of cliffs, headlands and beautiful views. As you cross the border you are scrutinized at a military border crossing and you may see the occasional army patrol on the road, but more than likely all you will see is mile after mile of glorious countryside.

Giant's Causeway

Yeats Country, County Donegal & the Giant's Causeway

The suggestion is that you plan an early afternoon arrival, giving you time for a stroll around SLIGO.   If you are an ardent admirer of the work of William Butler Yeats you will want to visit the County Museum which has a special section about his poetry and writing.   You may also wish to spend several days visiting the places about which he wrote so vividly.

RECOMMENDED LODGING

Simple accommodations are usually associated with farmhouses, but this is not the case at COOPERSHILL FARMHOUSE near RIVERSTOWN where almost all the beds are grand four-posters and antiques and demure family portraits are everywhere.

Barbara and Andrew Greenstein came here from America with their dog Poteen when they bought DRUMLEASE GLEBE HOUSE near DROMAHAIR. Every evening they gather with guests before and after dinner, creating a cozy house party atmosphere. The house is beautifully decorated and cherished antiques grace every nook and cranny. Three donkeys grazing in the field beyond the swimming pool complete the serene countryside picture.

Bed and breakfast accommodation is offered at DROMAHAIR'S local pub, the STANFORD VILLAGE INN. As is the case everywhere in Ireland, the pub plays an important part in village life. Tom and Della have kept the original bar just the way it always was, with its tall hard stools and fiddles hanging ready for someone to strike up a tune. A larger bar has been added in keeping with the traditional one. Upstairs the bedrooms offer a quiet night's sleep.

DESTINATION I   BRUCKLESS

Leave Sligo travelling north along the N15 to DRUMCLIFF CHURCHYARD, which has to be the most visited graveyard in Ireland - William Butler Yeats is buried here under the epitaph he composed, "Cast a cold eye on life, on death. Horseman pass by!" In the background is the imposing Benbulben Mountain, a familiar sight in the Sligo area.

Leaving the churchyard, return towards Sligo and at RATHCORMACK turn left through the village of DRUM to join the N16 as it travels east towards ENNISKILLEN. After checking with the guard at the border post, take the first turn to your right and follow signposts to MARBLE ARCH CAVES. This extensive network of limestone chambers billed as "over 300 million years of history" is most impressive. The tour includes an underground boat journey and walks through large illuminated chambers and galleries hung with remarkable stalactites. Remember to dress warmly and take a sweater. (The caves are open from March to October.)

Leaving the hilltop cave complex, follow signposts for Enniskillen. Do not go into the town but turn left along the A46, following the scenic southern shore of LOUGH ERNE (a huge island-studded paradise for birds and fishermen) to BELLEEK. Traditional methods for making pottery are still adhered to at the BELLEEK POTTERY where ivory-toned porcelain is festooned with shamrocks or delicate spaghetti-like strands woven into trellis-like plates. You can tour the factory, chat to the friendly workers and then shop at the factory shop.

Crossing back into the Republic, follow the N15 north to DONEGAL. The town is laid out around a diamond-shaped area where several very pleasant shops sell a wide variety of Donegal tweed items. The ruins of Donegal Castle (not open to the public), built in the 16th century by Hugh O'Donell, remain overlooking the river.

RECOMMENDED LODGING

From Donegal town it is a 12-mile drive west (N56) to BRUCKLESS HOUSE near BRUCKLESS. Clive and Joan Evans and their children came here from Hong Kong where Clive had for many years been a Senior Superintendent in the Hong Kong Police force. Their graceful Georgian home is within yards of the ocean. Horseriding is available if you make arrangements in advance.

Nearby KILLYBEGS is one of Ireland's major fishing ports. As you move west the landscape becomes more rugged and the signposts less frequent and, to complicate things, are written in Irish (Irish names are referenced in parentheses). KILCAR is a centre for Donegal handwoven tweeds and it's a short drive from here to CARRICK (AN CHARRAIG). Leaving Carrick, the road to GLENCOLUMB-KILLE (GLEANN CHOLAIM CILLE) enters the Owenwee Valley where you climb more than 600 feet before descending into the glen. Drive through the scattered village to GLENCOLUMBKILLE FOLK VILLAGE MUSEUM at the water's edge. Glencolumbkille is a very special place that gives an appreciation of the survival of a people who endured hardship, famine and debilitating emigration.

By the 1960s emigration was threatening to turn Glencolumbkille into a ghost town. In an effort to try and create some jobs the parish priest, Father McDyer, formed a cooperative of the remaining local residents to develop a tourist industry by building a folk museum and holiday homes and by encouraging local crafts. Father McDyer continues to assist in the running of his parish's cooperative and is often on hand to chat with visitors.

Tucked against a rocky hillside, the cottages that comprise the folk museum are grouped to form a traditional tiny village, or "clachan". Each cottage is a replica of those lived in by local people in each of three successive centuries. The thick thatched roofs are tied down with heavy rope and anchored with stones, securing them from the harsh Atlantic winds. Inside, the little homes are furnished with period furniture and utensils. Friendly locals guide you through the houses and give you snippets of local history. A handicraft shop sells Irish cottage crafts and the adjacent tearoom serves oven-fresh scones and piping hot tea on lovely Irish pottery.

Leaving Glencolumbkille, the narrow road climbs and dips through seemingly uninhabited rugged countryside where the views are often obscured by swirlings mists as you climb the Glengesh Pass before dropping down into ARDARA.

The road skirts the coast and brings you to the twin fishing villages of PORTNOO and NAIRN set amongst isolated beaches that truly have an "end-of-the-earth" quality about them. A short drive brings you to MAAS whence you travel an extremely twisty road to the Gweebarra bridge which brings you to LETTERMACAWARD (LEITIR MHIC AN BHAIRD) and on to DUNGLOW (AN GLOBHAN LIATH). Nearby in BURTONPORT (AILT AN CHORAIN) more salmon and lobster are landed than at any other port. From here you drive north to KINCASSLAGH and then it's on to ANNAGARY, GWEEDORE (GAOTH DOBHAIR) and FALCARRAGH (FAL CARRACH), communities that pride themselves on speaking the Irish language. A combination of wild, untamed scenery, villages that seem untouched by the 20th century and narrow, curving roads in general disrepair gives the feeling that the passage of time stopped many years ago in this isolated corner of Ireland.

From Falcarragh you come along the N56 to DUNFANAGHY. On the hill above the village sits THE GALLERY, one of Ireland's best antique, crafts and painting shops set in a Georgian country home. This is a most worthwhile stop in an area that is rich in scenery but where there are few things to visit. Driving becomes easier as the N56 approaches LETTERKENNY. Do not enter the town but turn left at the traffic island, following signposts for RAMELTON and RATHMULLAN.

RECOMMENDED LODGING

ARDEEN in RAMELTON offers bed and breakfast accommodation in a fine Victorian home overlooking the River Lennon. The four large bedrooms share the facilities of an equally spacious bathroom. A large garden sprawls in front of the house and there is a tennis court for guests' use.

Several miles to the north, RATHMULLAN HOUSE in RATHMULLAN offers spacious country house accommodation in a rambling 18th-century mansion. Bedroom decor varies between country house traditional and rather mis-matched modern. A series of lounges, dining rooms, library and a cellar bar are amongst the many large public rooms. The hotel's greatest asset is its gorgeous garden which slopes to the shores of Lough Swilly.

If you decide to seek more Donegal coastal landscape, then a day spent circling the FANAD and INISHOWEN peninsulas should give you what you need.

DESTINATION III   COLERAINE

GLENVEAGH NATIONAL PARK lies about an hour's drive from Rathmullan and Ramelton. It is well signposted across the purple heather-covered moorlands that lead to the picturesque glen surrounding Glenveagh Castle and its exquisite gardens. Leave your car at the Visitors' Centre and take the mini bus around the lake to the castle and its gardens. The heather and rose gardens, the rhododendrons, the laurels and pines, busts and statues are all lovingly maintained, but the walled kitchen garden is especially memorable, with its profusion of flowers and tidy rows of vegetables divided by narrow grass walkways. Surrounding this oasis of cultivated beauty are thousands of acres of wild countryside where the largest herd of red deer in Ireland roam.

Glenveagh Castle was built in 1870 by John Adair, using his American wife's money, to a fanciful Gothic design that was popular in the later part of the century. The rooms have been beautifully restored and for a small entrance fee you can tour the house. The Glenveagh estate was given to the nation by the castle's second owner, Henry McIlhenny, who is largely responsible for the design of the gardens. An audio visual program and displays at the Visitors' Centre explain the castle and its surrounding habitat. Cafes at the castle and the centre serve especially good food.

Leaving the national park, turn right across the desolate boglands and heather-clad hills - your destination is GLEBE GALLERY (4 miles away) near the village of CHURCH HILL. Derek Hill gave his home, Glebe House, and his art collection to the state who remodeled the outbuildings to display his fine collection of paintings by predominantly Irish artists.

From the gallery it is a 10-mile drive to LETTERKENNY. From the town your route into Northern Ireland is well signposted to DERRY, with stops at customs and the army checkpoint - the only reminders that you are crossing from Eire to Ulster. The N13 becomes the A2 as you cross the border and pounds sterling become the currency. Skirt Derry city on the FOYLE BRIDGE. Follow the A2 to LIMAVADY and the A37 for 13 miles to the outskirts of Coleraine where you take the A29 (signposted for COOKSTOWN and GARVAGH) to the following highly recommended places to stay near COLERAINE.

RECOMMENDED LODGING

BLACKHEATH HOUSE, once a rectory, was acquired by Joseph and Margaret Erwin as a family home in 1978 and later converted to a restaurant and country house hotel. Guests dine in MacDuff's, the intimate basement restaurant, and enjoy the comfort of the elegant, well furnished lounge. The bedrooms are smart and have color television and en-suite bathrooms.

Elizabeth Hegarty offers such a warmth of welcome and GREENHILL HOUSE is so very comfortable that guests who come for a couple of nights often return the following year for a longer holiday. Elizabeth thoroughly enjoys looking after visitors and this is reflected in the food she cooks (plan on sampling each of the four mouthwatering desserts that conclude dinner), the thoughtful little extras that she places in the bedrooms and the care she takes to help visitors plan their shopping and sightseeing trips. All the bedrooms are very nicely decorated and two of them enjoy en-suite bathrooms. Late in the evening guests gather around the sitting room fire to make new friends and enjoy a cup of tea and homemade cakes.

As you set out to explore the Causeway coast remember to take a sweater, for the blustery Atlantic winds chill even the warmest of days. Bushmills and the Giant's

Causeway are well signposted from the outskirts of Coleraine. (One of the delights of travelling in Northern Ireland is that the roads are well paved and the signposting frequent and accurate.) BUSHMILLS is famous for its whiskey - a whiskey spelt with an "e" - of which Special Old Black Bush is the best. A tour of the factory demonstrates how they turn barley and water into whiskey and rewards you with a sample of the classic drink to fortify you for your visit to the nearby Giant's Causeway. (Tours are offered on weekdays - call 31521 to make an appointment.)

In the last century the GIANT'S CAUSEWAY was thought to be one of the wonders of the world. Formed from basaltic rock which cooled and split into regular prismatic shapes, it stepped out to sea to build an irregular honeycomb of columns some 70,000,000 years ago. More romantic than scientific fact is the legend that claims the causeway was built by the Irish giant Finn MacCool to get at his rival in Scotland. Do not expect the columns to be tall - for they are not. It is their patterns that make them interesting, not their size.

The first stop on a visit to the Causeway is the Visitors' Centre where the facts and legends about the Causeway are well presented in an audio visual theatre. A mini bus takes you to the head of the causeway where you follow the path past formations called "Honeycomb", "Wishing Well", "Giant's Granny", "King and his Nobles", "Port na Spaniagh" (where gold and silver treasure from the Spanish Armada ship Girona was found in 1967), "Lovers' Leap" and up the wooden staircase to the headlands where you walk back to the Visitors' Centre along the clifftops. (It's a 5-mile walk and you can truly say you have seen the causeway if you complete the circuit.)

Leaving the Causeway, turn right along the coast to visit the ruins of the nearby DUNLUCE CASTLE, a romantic ruin clinging to a wave-lashed cliff with a great cave right underneath. This was the main fort of the Irish MacDonnells, chiefs of Antrim, and fell into the ruin after the kitchen (and cooks) fell into the sea during a storm.

Return to the Causeway gates and turn left along the coast road. Watch carefully for a small plaque at the side of the road pointing out the very meagre ruins of DUNSEVERICK CASTLE. Dunseverick was at the northermost end of the Celtic road where the Celts crossed to and from Scotland.

Shortly after joining the A2, turn left for PORT BRADON. The road winds down to the sea where a hamlet of gaily painted houses and a church nestle around a sheltered harbour. As you stand in front of the smallest church in Ireland, the long sandy beaches of WHITEPARK BAY stretch before you.

Farther along the coast a narrow road winds down to the very picturesque BALLINTOY HARBOUR, a sheltered haven for boats surrounded by small, jagged, rocky islands.

At the first road bend after leaving BALLINTOY village, turn sharp left for the CARRICK-A-REDE ROPE BRIDGE. This is one of the famous things to do in Ireland: walk 80 feet above the sea across a narrow, swinging bridge of planks and ropes that joins a precipitous cliff to a rocky island. Hardy fishermen whose cottages and nets nestle in a sheltered cleft on the island and whose fragile wooden boats bob in the ocean below still use the bridge.

Life in the nearby holiday town of BALLYCASTLE centres around the beach, fishing and golf. Cross the river and turn onto the A2 to BALLYVOY. If the weather is clear, turn left for the scenic drive to CUSHENDUN and TORR HEAD. The narrow road, barely wide enough for two cars to pass, switchbacks across the headlands and corkscrews down the cliffside, offering spectacular views of the rugged coastline and the distant village of Cushendun.

Leaving Cushendun, the landscape softens and the road, thankfully, returns to a more manageable width. You are now entering the GLENS OF ANTRIM where lush green fields and a succession of beautiful views present themselves. At

CUSHENDALL you can detour into GLENARIFF FOREST PARK, the queen of the glens with a series of waterfalls plunging down a gorge traversed by a scenic path crossing rustic bridges. Thackeray described this glen as "Switzerland in miniature".

Returning to the coast road, CARNLOUGH, a pretty seaside and fishing town, soon comes into view, its little white harbour full of bobbing boats. Limestone cliffs present themselves as you approach LARNE, a sizeable seaport whose Viking origins are lost amongst more modern commercial developments.

As the evening shadows lengthen, turn inland from the beautiful Antrim coast following the A36 to BALLYMENA (20 miles) and the A26 to COLERAINE and either Blackheath House or Greenhill House.

On your return to the Republic consider travelling as far as possible through Northern Ireland simply because the roads are excellent and the miles fly by. You may see soldiers patrolling the towns and the occasional tank, but other than that you'll see tranquil rolling countryside. As you travel south consider visiting the ULSTER-AMERICAN FOLK PARK, near OMAGH. Northern Ireland claims that 11 American presidents have their roots in County Tyrone and the park tells the story of the great migrations of Ulster people to the New World. All the cottages and old buildings in the park contain furniture, cooking utensils and farm implements. In the summer costumed blacksmiths, weavers, spinners and candlemakers bring the exhibits to life.

Glencolumbkille

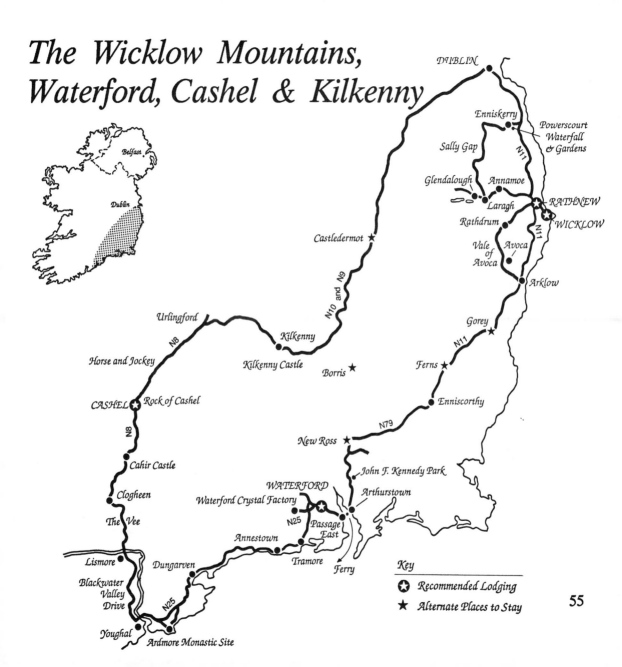

The Wicklow Mountains, Waterford, Cashel & Kilkenny

Belfast

Dublin

DUBLIN

Enniskerry

Powerscourt
Waterfall
& Gardens

Sally Gap

N11

Glendalough   Annamoe

Laragh   RATHNEW

Rathdrum   WICKLOW

Vale
of
Avoca   Avoca

N11

Castledermot

Arklow

N10 and N9

Gorey

Urlingford   Kilkenny   N11

N8   Kilkenny Castle   Ferns

Horse and Jockey   Borris   Enniscorthy

CASHEL   Rock of Cashel   N79

N8   New Ross

Cahir Castle   John F. Kennedy Park

Clogheen   WATERFORD   Arthurstown

The Vee   Waterford Crystal Factory

N25   Annestown   Passage
East

Lismore   Dungarvan   Tramore

Blackwater   Ferry
Valley
Drive   N25

Key

Youghal   Ardmore Monastic Site

⭐ *Recommended Lodging*

★ *Alternate Places to Stay*

55

The Wicklow Mountains, Waterford, Cashel & Kilkenny

All too often visitors rush from Dublin through Waterford and on to western Ireland, never realizing that they are missing some of the most ancient antiquities and lovely scenery along the seductive little byways that traverse the moorlands and wind through wooded glens.   This itinerary makes a loop from Dublin, pausing to admire the lovely Powerscourt Gardens, lingering amongst the ancient monastic ruins of Glendalough, visiting the Avoca handweavers who capture the subtle hues of heather and field in their fabric, admiring the skill of the Waterford cutters who turn raw glass into sparkling crystal, pausing to admire Ireland's tribute to President John F. Kennedy, climbing the massive Rock of Cashel, the ancient citadel of Irish kings, and visiting Kilkenny, the most attractive of medieval Irish towns.

Rock of Cashel

DUBLIN is the Republic of Ireland's capital, a beguiling blend of olde-worlde European and modern, regrettably scarred by the destruction of many of its old buildings. It's a bustling, vibrant city that invites discovery of its buildings, pubs, shops, gardens and, above all, its friendly people. Suggestions on what to see and do are covered in detail beginning on page 68.

DESTINATION I   RATHNEW or WICKLOW

The drive today is short, the first night's destination purposely chosen to allow you ample time to enjoy the interesting sights en route. Leave Dublin following the N11 in the direction of Wexford. (If you experience difficulty finding the correct road, follow signs for the ferry at Dun Laoghaire and from there pick up signs for Wexford.) As soon as the city suburbs are behind you, watch for signs indicating a right turn to POWERSCOURT GARDENS and ENNISKERRY. Follow the winding wooded lane to Enniskerry and bear left in the centre of the village: this brings you to the main gates of Powerscourt Gardens. As you drive through the vast parklike grounds, the mountains of Wicklow appear before you decked in every shade of green. Unfortunately, Powerscourt House was burnt to a ruin in 1974: a rook's nest blocked one of the chimneys and when a fire was lit in the fireplace the resultant blaze quickly engulfed this grand home.

The gardens descend in grand tiers from the ruined house, rather as if descending into a bowl - a mirror-like lake sits at the bottom. Masses of roses adorn the walled garden and velvet green grassy walks lead through the woodlands. Many visitors are intrigued by the animal cemetery with its little headstones and inscriptions. Such a corner is not uncommon in Irish stately homes.

Leaving the car park turn left for the 4-mile drive to the foot of POWERSCOURT WATERFALL, the highest waterfall in Ireland and a favorite summer picnic place for many Dubliners.

Turn to the left as you leave the waterfall grounds to meander along narrow country lanes towards GLENCREE. As you come upon open moorland take the first turn left for the 5-mile uphill drive to the summit of SALLY GAP. This road is known as the old military road because it follows the path that the British built across these wild mountains to aid them in their attempts to suppress the feisty men of County Wicklow. Neat stacks of turf are piled to dry in the sun and the wind. Grazing sheep seem to be the only occupants of this vast rolling moorland. Below GLENMACNASS WATERFALL the valley opens up to a patchwork of fields beckoning you to LARAGH and GLENDALOUGH.

Glendalough was built by Saint Kevin in the 6th century - a monastic settlement of seven churches. After Saint Patrick, Saint Kevin is Ireland's most popular saint. He certainly picked a stunning site in this wooded valley between two lakes to found his monastic order. Amidst the tilting stones of the graveyard, the round tower punctuates the skyline - still perfect after more than a thousand years. Leaving the monastery, continue up the narrow road until it dead-ends at the Upper Lake. Tradition has it that Saint Kevin lived a solitary life in a hut near here. Farther up on a cliff face is a cave known as St Kevin's Bed. Here, so the story goes, Kathleen a beautiful temptress tried to seduce him. To cool her advances he threw her into the lake.

As evening shadows lengthen, retrace the road to Laragh, turn left to ANNAMOE (2 1/2 miles), cross the bridge and turn right to ASHFORD (7 miles) where you join the N11 going south.

RECOMMENDED LODGING

Closest at hand near RATHNEW lies HUNTER'S HOTEL, one of the few traditional hostelries in Ireland. A quiet, old-fashioned atmosphere pervades the place, with the soft ticking of the hall clock marking the passage of time. The bedrooms are decorated with a country flavor that matches the cozy country feel of the house and blends perfectly with the flower-filled gardens. The very nicest rooms are those with en-suite bathrooms.

Just a few miles down the road on the other side of RATHNEW lies TINAKILLY HOUSE, where beautiful decor, lovely furniture, superb food and a warm welcome combine to make this one of Ireland's premier country house hotels.

If a country farmhouse is to your liking you can do no better than extend your journey the several miles to LISSADELL HOUSE near WICKLOW. Otto and Patricia Klaue's home has a very welcoming feel to it. Otto came here from East Germany many years ago and Patricia has learnt to cook many German dishes, offering them along with traditional Irish fare to her guests. Two of the bedrooms have private bathrooms and one offers a king sized bed.

The Wicklow Mountains, Waterford, Cashel & Kilkenny   59

Travel southwest from Rathnew to RATHDRUM.   As you head south through the VALE OF AVOCA to the "Meeting of the Waters", at the confluence of the rivers Avonmore and Avonbeg, the scenery is lovely.   Detour into AVOCA to visit the handweavers.   You are welcome to wander amongst the skeins and bobbins of brightly hued wool to see the weavers at work and talk to them above the noise of the looms.   An adjacent shop sells tweeds and woolens.

At ARKLOW join the N11, a broad, fast road taking you south through GOREY and FERNS to ENNISCORTHY.   Amidst the gray stone houses built on steeply sloping ground by the River Slaney lies a Norman castle.   Rebuilt in 1586, the castle houses a folk museum and has lots of information about Wexford's part in the 1798 rising against English rule.

Just after the N79 merges with the N25 turn left for Arthurstown and the JOHN F. KENNEDY PARK.   The great-grandfather of American President John F. Kennedy emigrated from nearby DUNGANSTOWN - driven from Ireland by the terrible potato famine of the 1840s.   Row upon row of dark evergreens stand before you like an honor guard to the slain president as you climb to the panoramic viewing point atop Slieve Coillte.

Return to the main road and continue south to ARTHURSTOWN where a small ferry takes you across the estuary to PASSAGE EAST, the tiny village on the eastern shores of Waterford Harbour.

Following signs for Waterford, a short drive brings you to the lodgings recommended for tonight's stay.

RECOMMENDED LODGING:

FOXMOUNT FARM, near WATERFORD, is a traditional farmhouse. Margaret enjoys cooking for her guests and uses beef, vegetables and fruits fresh from the farm. She particularly enjoys making desserts, with homemade ice cream her specialty.

Just a little farther down the WATERFORD road you come to THE OLD COACH HOUSE, one of my very favorite Irish country inns. Liz and Michael have such a natural non-fussy way of m ... you feel right at home and Liz does a splendid job with the food, offering her guests an extremely good four course dinner. The house is in decorator-perfect order and you may be tempted to forget the rest of your plans and readjust your holiday to stay here longer.

CLOSED

DESTINATION III   CASHEL

If you are intensely interested in the production or are an avid collector of Waterford crystal ask Foxmount Farm or The Old Coach House to secure you a reservation on a tour of the nearby WATERFORD CRYSTAL FACTORY. (Tours are offered on weekdays five times a day from 10.15am to 2.30pm by appointment only.) If you do not have an appointment you can see the hand-blowing and cutting of sparkling crystal on a video presentation. The adjacent showroom displays the full line of Waterford's production from shimmering chandeliers to glassware. There are no seconds and Waterford crystal items are uniformly priced throughout the country.

From the factory double back in the direction of Waterford for a very short distance, turning to the right to TRAMORE, a family holiday town, long a favorite of the ice cream and bucket and spade brigade. Skirting the town, follow the beautiful coastal road through ANNESTOWN to DUNGARVEN.

Where the coastal road meets the N25 make a detour from your route turning sharp left to SHELL HOUSE - like it or hate it, there is nothing quite like it on any suburban street in the world - a cottage where all available wall surfaces are decorated in colored shells in various patterns. Ring the bell to tour the garden and you will probably be invited in to view shell souvenirs. Their sale aids leper colonies in Africa and their purchase certainly celebrates the ingenuity that went into creating the yard.

Returning to the main road after crossing Dungarven Harbour, the N25 winds up and away from the coast presenting lovely views of the town and the coast. If you haven't eaten, try SEANACHIE (a restored thatched farmhouse, now a traditional restaurant and bar) which sits atop the hill and serves good Irish and Continental food.

After passing through several miles of forested plantings, turn left on the R673 to ARDMORE, following the coastline to the village. Beyond the neatly painted houses that cluster together lies the ARDMORE MONASTIC SITE. The well preserved round tower used to have six internal timber landings which were joined by ladders, and at the top was a bell to call the monks to prayer or warn of a hostile raid. The round tower is unique to Ireland, its entrance door placed well above the ground: entry was gained by means of a ladder which could be drawn up whenever necessary. Early Christian monks built round towers as protection against Vikings and other raiders.

Leaving the ruins, turn left in the village, following signs for YOUGHAL. (This itinerary does not go into the town - pronounced "you all" with an American Southern drawl - but it is interesting to note that Sir Walter Raleigh who introduced the potato and tobacco was once its mayor. It's a pleasant old town whose one-way traffic system makes it impossible to explore without parking the car and walking.) Cross the River Blackwater and at the end of the bridge turn sharp right on BLACKWATER VALLEY DRIVE, a narrow road which follows the broad muddy waters of the Blackwater through scenic wooded countryside. The "drive" is well signposted as SCENIC ROUTE. Quiet country roads bring you into LISMORE. Turn left into town and right at the town square. Cross the river and take the second road to the left, following signs for CLOGHEEN and THE VEE. As the road climbs, woods give way to heathery moorlands climbing to the summit where the valley opens before you - a broad "V" shape framing an endless patchwork of fields in every shade of green.

CAHIR CASTLE has stood on guard to defend the surrounding town of CAHIR since 1375. A guided tour explains the elaborate defensive system, making a visit here both interesting and informative. A separate audio visual presentation provides information about the castle and other monuments in the area.

Leaving the castle, continue through the town square for the 10-mile drive to CASHEL. The ROCK OF CASHEL seems to grow out of the landscape as you near the town and you can see why this easily defensible site was the capital for the kings of Munster as long ago as 370 AD. In the course of converting Ireland to Christianity, Saint Patrick reached the castle, and according to legend, jabbed his staff into the king's foot during the conversion ceremony. The king apparently took it all very stoically, thinking it was part of the ritual.

Upon reaching the summit of the rock, you find a 10th-century round tower, 13th-century cathedral and 15th-century entrance building or Hall of Vicars Choral, a building that was sensitively restored in the 1970s and now houses some exhibits including Saint Patrick's Cross, an ancient Irish high cross of unusual design.

RECOMMENDED LODGING

Overlooking the Rock of Cashel on the town's main street, within easy walking distance of the shops, stands *CASHEL PALACE*, once the opulent home of the local bishop. The principal bedrooms are luxurious rooms of grand proportions, while smaller bedrooms are tucked into what were once the servants' quarters under the eaves. Elegant dining is offered in the Four Seasons Restaurant. The Bishop's Buttery, in the old cellars, serves less elaborate food in informal surroundings.

Nine miles to the northeast at *HORSE AND JOCKEY* (listed Cashel), beside the pub and restaurant of the same name, sits *PARKSTOWN HOUSE*. This splendid Georgian home is in absolutely tiptop condition. Several pieces of grand gilt furniture grace the public rooms with displays of family silver and crystal adorning the dining room. Upstairs the bedrooms are beautifully decorated. The master bedroom and adjacent twin room can be combined to form a suite with a private bathroom. Parkstown House provides such a comfortable place to stay that an intended stay of one night usually extends to several.

(Rather than return to Dublin you can take today's proposed journey to Kilkenny as a daytrip from Cashel and then proceed west, joining the KILLARNEY, KINSALE & THE WESTERN PENINSULAS itinerary in Kinsale and reversing it to follow the coast westward through Bantry and around the Ring of Kerry to Killarney, Dingle and Shannon Airport.)

Leave Cashel on the N8 for the 25-mile drive northeast to URLINGFORD where you bear right for the 17-mile drive to KILKENNY.   Kilkenny is quite the loveliest of Irish towns and it will be easy to spend most of the day here before returning to Dublin.   Entering the town, turn left at the first traffic lights along the main street and park your car outside the castle.

KILKENNY CASTLE was first built between 1195 and 1207.   The imposing building as it now stands is a mixture of Tudor and Gothic design and is definitely worth a visit.   The east wing picture gallery is flooded by natural light from the skylit roof and displays a collection of portraits of the Ormonde family, the owners of Kilkenny castle from 1391 until 1967.

Opposite the castle entrance, the stables now house the KILKENNY DESIGN CENTRE, a retail outlet for goods of Irish design and production: silver jewelry, knits, textiles, furniture and crafts.

Undoubtedly the best way to see the medieval buildings of Kilkenny is on foot.   A walking tour starts from the Tourist Office in the SHEE ALMS HOUSE just a short distance from the castle.

Stroll up High Street into Parliament Street to ROTHE HOUSE.   The house, built in 1594 as the home of Elizabethan merchant John Rothe, is now a museum depicting how such a merchant lived.

You should also see SAINT CANICE'S CATHEDRAL at the top of Parliament Street. The round tower dates from the 6th century when Saint Canice founded a monastic order here. Building began on the cathedral in 1251, though most of the lovely church you see today is an 1864 restoration.

Alleyways with such fanciful names as The Butter Slip lead you from the High Street to Saint Kieran Street where you find KYLTERS INN, the oldest building in town. This historic inn has a lurid history - supposedly a hostess of many centuries ago murdered four successive husbands, was then accused of witchcraft and narrowly escaped being burnt at the stake by fleeing to the Continent.

A 64-mile drive along the N10 and N9 returns you to DUBLIN.

Dublin Walking Tour

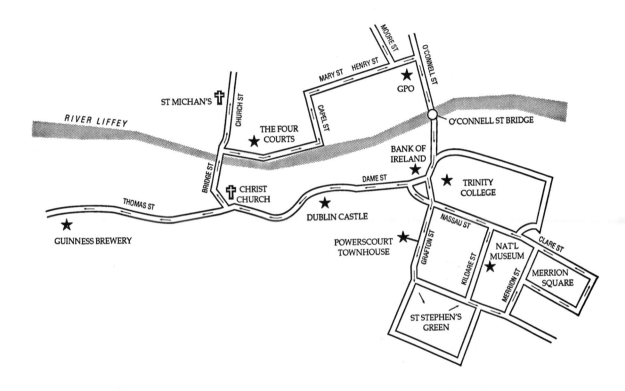

RIVER LIFFEY

ST MICHAN'S

CHURCH ST

MOORE ST

O'CONNELL ST

MARY ST   HENRY ST

CAPEL ST

GPO

O'CONNELL ST BRIDGE

THE FOUR COURTS

BANK OF IRELAND

BRIDGE ST

CHRIST CHURCH

DAME ST

TRINITY COLLEGE

THOMAS ST

DUBLIN CASTLE

NASSAU ST

CLARE ST

GUINNESS BREWERY

POWERSCOURT TOWNHOUSE

GRAFTON ST

KILDARE ST

NAT'L MUSEUM

MERRION ST

MERRION SQUARE

ST STEPHEN'S GREEN

Dublin Walking Tour

"In Dublin's fair city where the girls are so pretty" goes the popular old ballad. The girls are certainly pretty and the city fair if you can overlook the rash of modern office developments begun in the 1960s and the large areas that have been razed and seemingly abandoned. Dublin now appears to have seen the error of its ways and efforts are being made to restore what the bulldozers have spared. A car is more trouble than it is worth in Dublin. If your visit here is at the outset of your trip, I suggest that you not get your car until you are ready to leave or, if Dublin is a stop on your trip, park it for the duration of your stay. Dublin is a walking town, so don comfortable shoes and set out to explore the buildings, streets, and shops of this bustling, friendly city. If you feel weary along the way there is no shortage of pubs full of atmosphere where you can revive yourself with a refreshing drink.

Georgian Doors

A convenient place to begin your tour is the O'CONNELL STREET BRIDGE which spans the River Liffey dividing the north from the south of Dublin. (It is also just by the city centre terminus for buses: those displaying "An Lar", meaning city centre, usually end up here.) Turn south into WESTMORLAND STREET past the sombre, windowless BANK OF IRELAND which began life in 1729 as the seat of Irish parliament. Cross the street and enter through the front arch of TRINITY COLLEGE into the square. Founded in 1591 by Elizabeth I, it contains a fine collection of buildings from the 18th to the 20th centuries. Cross the square to the OLD LIBRARY where the "Book of Kells" is displayed. A page of this magnificent illuminated manuscript dating from about 800 AD is turned every month and if you are not overly impressed by the page on display, return to the library bookshop and browse through a reproduction.

Retrace your steps to the front gate and turn south into GRAFTON STREET which is closed to vehicles and teems with people. Its large modern department store SWITZERS and the more traditional store BROWN & THOMPSON are popular places to shop. JOHNSTON'S COURT, a narrow lane, leads you to POWERSCOURT TOWNHOUSE, a collection of small shops under the roof of Viscount Powerscourt's former townhouse. Returning to Grafton Street, let yourself be tempted into BEWLEY'S CAFE, a landmark old-fashioned tea and coffee shop frequented by Dubliners. Upstairs genteel waitress service is offered while downstairs it's self service of tea, coffee, sticky buns, sausages, chips and the like. The food is not outstanding but the atmosphere is very Dublin.

At the end of Grafton Street dodge the hurrying buses and cross into the peaceful tranquility of ST STEPHEN'S GREEN, an island of flowers, trees and grass surrounding small lakes dotted with ducks.

Return to the northern side of the square past the landmark SHELBOURNE HOTEL into MERRION ROW. Turn left into MERRION STREET (the Duke of Wellington, who defeated Napoleon at the Battle of Waterloo, was born at number 24) which brings you to MERRION SQUARE, one of Dublin's finest remaining

Georgian squares and the onetime home of several famous personages - William Butler Yeats lived at 82 and earlier at 52, Daniel O'Connell at 51 and Oscar Wilde's parents occupied number 1.

Stroll around the square into CLARE STREET, stopping to browse in GREENE'S BOOKSTORE with its lovely old facade and tables of books outside. (If you still have energy, detour into KILDARE STREET to visit the NATIONAL LIBRARY, LEINSTER HOUSE, home of the modern day parliament, and the NATIONAL MUSEUM.) Follow the rails of Trinity College to KILKENNNY DESIGN CENTRE and BLARNEY WOOLEN MILLS, fine places to shop for Irish crafts and clothing.

With your back to the front gate of Trinity College, cross into DAME STREET where the statue of Henry Gratton, a famous orator, stands with his arms outstretched outside his parliament building. Walk along Dame Street past one of Dublin's less controversial modern buildings, the CENTRAL BANK. The street rises slightly as you pass into what was medieval Dublin which grew up around DUBLIN CASTLE. Built on the site of an earlier Danish fortification the castle was built in the early 13th century. The adjoining 18th-century STATE APARTMENTS with their ornate furnishings are more impressive inside than out.

Returning to Dame Street you pass CITY HALL and on your right the impressive CHRIST CHURCH CATHEDRAL comes into view. Dedicated in 1192, it has been rebuilt and restored many times. After the Reformation when Protestant religion was imposed on the Irish people it became a Protestant cathedral (Church of Ireland). The large crypt remained as a gathering spot and marketplace for the locals (Catholics) who used it for many years until a rector expelled them because their rowdiness was interrupting church services. Another point of interest is Stongbow's tomb: he was one of the most famous kings of Ireland and by tradition debts were paid across his tomb. When a wall collapsed and crushed this a replacement unknown crusader's tomb was conscripted and named Strongbow's tomb.

FISHAMBLE, the street where Molly Malone "wheeled her wheelbarrow" winds down to the River Liffey along the east side of the cathedral. During recent excavations for the modern civic offices the remains of WOOD QUAY, a Viking town, were unearthed. Despite a public campaign for the preservation and reconstruction of this invaluable archaeological site, building went ahead on the bunker-like civic offices.

At the junction of High Street and Bridge Street pause to climb the restored remains of a portion of DUBLIN'S WALLS. When they were built in 1240 the walls fronted onto the River Liffey.

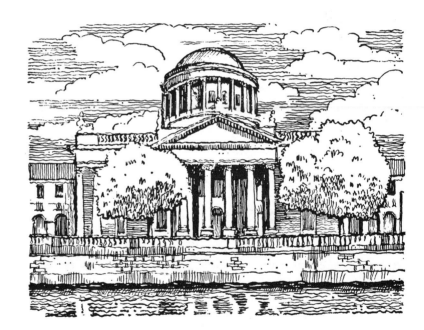

The Four Courts

If you feel like walking the distance along THOMAS STREET now is the time to detour about half a mile to that thriving Dublin institution the GUINNESS BREWERY, whence flows the national drink. As you near your goal the smell of roasting grains permeates the air. Entering the Guinness hop store, your reward for watching an audio-visual show on the making of the world famous Irish brew is a sample (pints if you wish) of the divine liquid and the chance to purchase souvenirs of all things Guinness. No, the 2,000,000 gallons of water a day that the brewery uses do not come from the Liffey but from St James's well on the Grand Canal - it is this limestone water that gives Guinness its characteristic flavor.

If you are not up to the walk, cross diagonally from the walls to the BRAZEN HEAD in BRIDGE STREET where you can enjoy that same brew in Dublin's oldest pub. There has been a tavern on this site since Viking times, though the present rather dilapidated premises date from 1688. It's always a crowded spot that really comes alive late in the evening when musicians gather for impromptu traditional music sessions.

Cross the River Liffey and if you are of a macabre turn of mind continue straight up CHURCH STREET to ST MICHAN'S CHURCH where the crypt's interred occupants have not decomposed because the limestone walls absorb moisture from the air. This grisly spectacle can be inspected and the sextant assured me that you can shake one of the occupant's hands.

Strolling along the INNS QUAY you come to THE FOUR COURTS, the supreme and high courts of Ireland. You can look inside the fine circular waiting hall under the beautiful green dome that allows light through its apex. If it is early morning you may see barristers in their gowns and wigs on their way to court.

Turn right up CAPEL STREET and third left into MARY STREET where little shops sell all manner of goods and lead to the busiest pedestrian shopping street in Dublin, HENRY STREET. Hardy ladies wrapped in warm woolen coats stand before their prams and bawl in Dublinese, "Bananas 6 for 50" and "Peaches 50 a basket". A short detour down MOORE STREET takes you through Dublin's colorful open-air fruit, veg and flower market.

On reaching O'CONNELL STREET turn right to the GENERAL POST OFFICE. The GPO, as it is affectionately known, is a national shrine because the headquarters of the 1916 revolution was here. O'Connell Street has its share of tourist traps and hamburger stores but it's a lively bunch of Dubliners who walk its promenades: placard-carrying nuns, nurses collecting for charity, hawkers of fruit, flowers and plastic trinkets all are there for you to see as you stroll this wide boulevard back to your starting point at O'Connell Street Bridge past the statues of those who fought for Ireland's freedom.

Accommodation in a modern bungalow is not the usual recommendation of this guide, but Adare is such a lovely village with its wide main street and quaint thatched cottages that I searched to find the very best guesthouse accommodations that it has to offer, and Abbey Villa is it.   Just off the main steet, on a quiet road of modern houses, Abbey Villa is a purpose-built guesthouse offering comfortable bedrooms each with a private bathroom.   There are three double and twin-bedded rooms and two large family rooms that overlook the small garden.   Mary Dundon offers no meals except breakfast but restaurants to suit every taste and budget are within walking distance.   Mary quite often finds herself fixing soup and a sandwich and pots of tea for her exhausted guests who arrive direct from their transatlantic flights to the nearby Shannon Airport.   The lounge provides a quiet place to sit and lots of information on the village and nearby attractions.   From Shannon Airport take the N18 to Limerick and the N20 to the N21 (Killarney road) to Adare - a 45-minute drive.   Pass the Dunraven Arms on your right, take the first right on Kildimo Road and Abbey Villa is the first house on your right.

ABBEY VILLA
Owner: Mary Dundon
Kildimo Road
Adare
Co Limerick
tel: (061) 86113
5 bedrooms with private bathrooms
£12 per person B & B
Open: all year
Credit cards: AX, MC, VS
Guesthouse

The Dunraven Arms stands on the broad main street of this neat village, its flower-filled garden adding to the picturesque scene.   With its uniformed staff and formal restaurant it has more the feel of a manor-hunting lodge than a hostelry.   The hotel is smartly decorated and attractive antique furniture adds to the olde-worlde feeling.   The bedrooms are prettily papered and have matching drapes and bedspreads, and rooms both front and back have lovely views of the gardens.   The large informal bar is the gathering place for locals and residents alike but if you want a few quiet moments there is a snug residents' lounge with chintz covered chairs gathered round a log fire.   The dining room has quite a reputation for its food - a laden dessert cart sits centre stage and waiters hover attentively.   If more informal dining is to your taste visit the hotel's cozy restaurant, "The Inn Between" in a quaint thatched cottage across the street.   Adare is on the N21, 25 miles from Shannon Airport, which makes it an ideal first or last stop in Ireland if you are coming from or going to the southwest.

DUNRAVEN ARMS
Manager: Bryan Murphy
Adare
Co Limerick
tel: (061) 86209
24 bedrooms with private bathrooms
From £36 single to £77 double
Open: all year
Credit cards: all major
U.S. Rep: R.S.I.
Rep tel: 800-223-1588
Country inn

The first impression of Ballycormac House is delightful: a sparkling white, 300-year-old cottage beyond green lawns bordered by flower-filled gardens. The interior is just as attractive - snug cottage rooms with pretty wallpapers and restful color schemes complemented by comfortable country antiques. Several bedrooms are at the top of narrow staircases, tucked under the beamed roof, so it's as well not to bring too much luggage. Rosetta is a cordon-bleu cook offering delicious dinners around the large antique pine refectory table. Every other week during the summer week-long trail rides are offered and from November to March you can enjoy foxhunting holidays - please call or write for brochures outlining these programs. If you do not ride or hunt you can venture out each day to such places as Bunratty Castle and Folk Park, Clonmacnois Abbey and Lough Derg, returning each night to your cozy country cottage. To find Ballycormac House follow the N52 northeast from Nenagh through Borrisokane to Ballingarry (15 miles) where you turn left for a 2-mile drive to Aglish.

BALLYCORMAC HOUSE
Owners: John & Rosetta Paxman
Aglish near Borrisokane
Nenagh
Co Tipperary
tel: (067) 21129
5 bedrooms with private bathrooms
£11 per person B & B
Open: all year
Credit cards: none
U.S. Rep: Fits Equestrian
Rep tel: 805-688-9494
Farmhouse

When Major Aldridge retired from the army in the 1930s he and his young bride Constance retired to Mount Falcon to enjoy the country life. Friends came to hunt, fish and visit and more than half a century later Constance continues to offer a hospitable welcome to visitors to her home. Guests help themselves to before-dinner drinks on the honor system from the bar in the alcove just off the dining room. A gong announces dinner and guests take their places at the long dining room table while Constance carves the roast and sits at head of table to enjoy dinner and conversation with her visitors, many of whom have become dear family friends over the span of years that they have returned to Mount Falcon. After dinner the convivial house party continues in the drawing room as guests recline in the comfortable chairs and sofas grouped around the blazing log fire. The bedrooms are large and airy, furnished in an old fashioned way, the decor a tad faded. Six have en-suite bathrooms while four have private bathrooms down the hall. Mount Falcon caters particularly to the angler and Constance and her fishery manager have extensive knowledge of both the 7 miles of the house's private beats along the River Moy and fishing in the area. From Ballina take the Foxford road south (N57) - the hotel is on your right 3 miles out of town.

MOUNT FALCON
Owner: Constance Aldridge
Ballina
Co Mayo
tel: (096) 21171 telex: 40899
10 bedrooms with private bathrooms
From £27.50 single to £110 double
Closed: Christmas, February & March
Credit cards: all major
U.S. Rep: Robert Reid, tel: 800-223-6510
Country house

This large rambling farmhouse was built at the turn of the century as a grand country residence. Raymond (who hails from Wales) and Violet Thomas came here to farm and subsequently opened their large home as a bed and breakfast. Over the years it has turned into a family operation: son Graham and his wife now manage the farm (they have a herd of gentle golden Jersey cows) and daughter Helen has returned from Europe to cook. The house has an airy spaciousness to it, with high beamed ceilings and large windows framing the surrounding countryside. An Oriental carpet adds a warmth to the living room where deep comfy chairs covered in chinz are grouped round the fire. A ceiling-wide skylight floods the hall and the staircase with light. Four of the bedrooms are enormous in size, the other two seeming small by comparison - all are plainly decorated. The bedrooms share two bathrooms. For those who are visiting relatives in the area, or need a base for a fishing holiday, Riversdale offers three small self-catering units in the courtyard. From Dublin take the N4 (Sligo road) to Dromod then turn right through Mohill to Ballinamore. In the centre of the village turn right by the church and Riversdale is on your left 1 1/2 miles out of town.

RIVERSDALE
Owners: The Thomas Family
Ballinamore
Co Leitrim
tel: (078) 44122
6 bedrooms sharing 2 bathrooms
£9 per person B & B
Open: all year
Credit cards: none
Farmhouse

Set on the shores of Lough Derg, the largest lake on the River Shannon, Gurthalougha House is a delightfully old-fashioned country home run with great enthusiasm by Michael and Bessie Wilkinson. Bessie is the daughter of one of Ireland's most famous hoteliers, Ken Besson, and Michael is a man who loves to cook. Between them they run a warm, welcoming place where there is no regimentation about meal hours. Dinner is as late or as early as you wish and breakfast is just about any time before dinner - served either in your bedroom or in the dining room. The food is wonderful, the wine is good and it's difficult to tear yourself away from the captivating charm of the place. The bedrooms are spacious in size but plainly decorated. The adjacent lough is an ideal place for fishermen, and even if you don't fish a delightul place to row. Paddy's Pub for a quiet pint and the Old Church Pottery for watching the potters at work make a visit to the nearby village of Terryglass worthwhile. Gurthalougha House is located 16 miles north of Nenagh (N52) between the villages of Terryglass and Ballinderry - the hotel is signposted in Ballinderry.

GURTHALOUGHA HOUSE
Owners: Michael & Bessie Wilkinson
Ballinderry near Borrisokane
Nenagh
Co Tipperary
tel: (067) 22080
8 bedrooms, 5 with private bathrooms
£25 per person B & B
Open: all year
Credit cards: none
Country house

This tall, bright white Victorian house is set amidst lush gardens that rim the shores of Bantry Bay. Although it is worth a stay here just to soak up the spectacular scenery, the house has much to offer. Kathleen O'Sullivan is a friendly and warm hostess who ensures not only that her guests are made to feel welcome but also that they are well fed - she has a deserved reputation for serving fine food in her lovely dining room. The menu is written every afternoon and based on what is fresh and available in the local market - the five courses offer plenty of choices and everything is cooked to order. The spacious bedrooms are individually decorated, those at the front of the house having the advantage of views of Bantry Bay through the trees. In addition, Kathleen has two very comfortable cottages on the grounds, just the place for families, friends travelling together or those who want to stay for an extended period. Sea View is Kathleen's family home, the atmosphere friendly and informal, which accounts, I am sure, for the large number of guests who return here year after year. Sea View House is located in Ballylickey on the N71 between Bantry and Glengarriff.

SEA VIEW HOUSE HOTEL
Owner: Kathleen O'Sullivan
Ballylickey
Co Cork
tel: (027) 50462/50073
8 bedrooms with private bathrooms
From £23 single to £52 double
Open: April to October
Credit cards: all major
U.S. Rep: R.S.I.
Rep tel: 800-223-1588
Country house

Gregan's Castle is only 45 miles from Shannon Airport, so if you are heading north this is the perfect spot to spend your first nights in Ireland. This is not an imposing castle but a sprawling manor house set in a lush green valley completely surrounded by the Burren, with its moonscapes of gray limestone and oases of Alpine and Arctic plants. The entire house is delightfully decorated. Public rooms include a snug library and a cozy lounge - blazing peat fires add a cheery warmth. The dining room, where Peter Haden supervizes the production of delectable food, frames an outstanding view across the Burren to the distant Galway Bay. My favorite room is the Corkscrew Bar, its blackened beams hung with copper and brass. Lunch is served here and in the evening guests and locals gather for a drink and a chat. Three luxurious suites have doors to the garden and are perfect for families or those seeking spacious quarters. The upstairs bedrooms are more modest in size, but comfortable and nicely decorated. From Shannon Airport take the N18 to Ennis, the N85 towards Ennistymon and the first right (R474) through Corofin. At the ruined Leamaneh Castle turn right, and as you crest the Burren you see Gregan's Castle in the valley below.

GREGAN'S CASTLE
Owners: Peter & Moira Haden
Ballyvaughan
Co Clare
tel: (065) 77005 telex: 70130
17 bedrooms, 14 with private bathrooms
From £48 single to £68 double
Open: Easter to October
Credit cards: VS
U.S. Rep: Robert Reid
Rep tel: 800-223-6510
Country house hotel

John and Mary Marnane have been welcoming visitors to their farm for over 20 years - Mary continues to offer a warm welcome with a cup of tea and encourages her guests to spend a couple of days with her so that she can get to know them and they can enjoy the peace and quiet of Irish farmhouse life. The seven simple bedrooms offer twin, double and family accommodation and share two bathrooms. Mary offers good farmhouse-style dinners to guests seated round the large dining room table. After dinner you can relax in the sitting room or take a walk down to the Marnanes' pub in the village. While the nearby town of Tipperary has little to offer the tourist there are several things to do and see in the area. The Glen of Aherlow is just a few miles away, and a magnificent view and woodland walks from "Christ the King Statue" make this a must. The Rock of Cashel, Hoare Abbey, Holy Cross Abbey and Cahir Castle are all within a 12-mile radius. From Tipperary take the Waterford road (N24) to Bansha, turn left in the village and the farm is on your right after half a mile.

BANSHA HOUSE
Owners: John & Mary Marnane
Bansha
near Tipperary
Co Tipperary
tel: (062) 54194
7 bedrooms sharing 2 bathrooms
£10 per person B & B
Open: all year
Credit cards: none
Farmhouse

Just as you arrive in Bantry town you see the entrance gate to Bantry House on your right. Dating from 1750, this stately home has fine views of the bay and, like so many grand Irish houses, is struggling to keep up its elegant buildings. The current descendant of the Earls of Bantry, Egerton Shellswell-White has restored a wing of the house in a more modern vein, offering bright airy rooms on a bed and breakfast basis. At the time of my visit, overnight guests took breakfast and dinner at a large pine refectory table set before the blackened kitchen range. In the daytime, this room doubles as a tea shop but construction is under way to add a more formal dining room in a remodeled wing. The main house is open to visitors who tour the baronial rooms with the aid of a typed sheet which explains the house's treasures on a room-by-room basis. In contrast to the grand formality of the house, the guestrooms are country cozy: large pastel decorated rooms where brass and iron bedsteads are topped by sprigged comforters. Bantry is on the N71 between Skibbereen and Kenmare.

BANTRY HOUSE
Owner: Egerton Shellswell-White
Bantry
Co Cork
tel: (027) 50047
10 bedrooms, 6 with private bathrooms
£15 per person B & B
Open: all year
Credit cards: none
Stately home

The Gables was built by the owner of nearby Blarney Castle for the parish priest and it served as a rectory until the Lynches purchased it as their family home in 1971.   Berna Lynch offers guests a friendly welcome to her home and provides lots of information on Blarney.   The Gables is most attractively decorated: lovely antique furniture graces the large dining room, the welcoming lounge and several of the bedrooms.   Accommodation is offered in two large family rooms with private bathrooms and showers and two smaller bedrooms which share a large old-fashioned bathroom with a huge tub.   There are many activities to occupy you in Blarney besides the obligatory visit to the castle to kiss the Blarney stone; an excellent riding school is five minutes way, golf fifteen minutes and the shopping in Blarney is excellent, with the stores staying open till dusk during the summer months.   There are several places to eat in town but if you make arrangements in advance Berna is happy to offer you a traditional Irish dinner.   The Gables is signposted on the outskirts of the village on the main Cork to Blarney road.   If you are arriving from Killarney drive through the village onto the Cork road and take the second turning to the left signposted for the Gables.

THE GABLES
Owner: Berna Lynch
Stoneview
Blarney
Co Cork
tel: (021) 385330
4 bedrooms, 2 with private bathrooms
From £10.50 to £12.50 per person B & B
Open: March to October
Credit cards: none
Country home

Bobbie Smith is a caring hostess carrying on the tradition of warm farmhouse hospitality started by her mother over 20 years ago. The house is the home of the Smiths and their three young daughters - books, games and family mementos are scattered all over the place and you soon feel at home. Children have an informal library/playroom to entertain themselves in if the weather is inclement and on fine days the outdoors offers lots to keep them busy - two playful dogs, (Mildred) the pet sheep, outdoor toys and a croquet lawn - and there are always the cows to watch as they come home every morning and evening to be milked. Bobbie learnt her cooking skills in the Australian outback catering to camping groups. The nearest she comes to a campfire meal these days is a summer barbeque in the garden - our supper was fresh grilled trout and salads, followed by coffee and conversation before the blazing fire in the lovely, old-fashioned drawing room. Ask for the bedroom with the large feather mattress: its comfort will surprise you. All rooms are attractively decorated with family antiques and furniture that Bobbie has bought at local auctions. Take the N9 from Dublin to Royal Oak (south of Carlow), turn left into Bagenalstown (Muine Bheag) and right in the village for the 4-mile drive to Lorum Old Rectory.

LORUM OLD RECTORY
Owner: Bobbie Smith
Kilgreaney, Bagenalstown
near Borris
Co Carlow
tel: (0503) 75282
5 bedrooms sharing 2 bathrooms
£10.50 per person B & B
Open: all year
Credit cards: DC, VS
Farmhouse

Step House is found opposite, and was formerly part of, the estate of the MacMurragh Kavanaghs - once Kings of Leinster. Breda's father purchased the house in 1930 and when he died in 1980 Breda returned armed with the culinary skills she had learned in London. The addition of three bedrooms means that guests can dine and stay in this delightful country village, making it their base for trips to Kilkenny and the surrounding countryside. Pre-dinner drinks and perusal of the menu are offered in the cozy piano bar before a blazing log fire. Dinner is by candlelight and Breda offers the choice between a short a la carte menu and an inclusive menu of the evening - her culinary success has earned her a 2-fork Michelin rating. Both the food and wine are excellent. Dinner is served from 7pm to 11pm, lunch is offered at the weekends and the restaurant is closed on Sunday and Monday evenings. A less formal bistro type restaurant and bar is being built in the basement with large French windows opening onto the garden. Upstairs accommodation is offered in two roomy twin-bedded rooms and a large front bedroom where a grand Victorian half tester bed sits centre stage. Borris is off the N9 (Waterford to Dublin road) from Dublin: turn left at Gowran (60 miles) for the 8-mile drive to Borris.

STEP HOUSE
Owner: Breda Coady
Borris
Co Carlow
tel: (0503) 73401
3 bedrooms with private bathrooms
From £15 to £20 per person B & B
Open: April to December
Restaurant closed Sundays & Mondays
Credit cards: VS
Restaurant with rooms

Bruckless House was built in the late 18th century by the Cassidy brothers, traders and merchants who took pickled herring from Donegal town, traded them for arms and ammunition in Sligo, then went on down to Portugal where they sold the guns to Napoleon and pickled herrings to Wellington.   Later the house was owned by a passionate communist, Commander Fjorde, who is remembered for his many good works in the area.   Both he and his wife are buried in the garden.   Continuing the tradition of owners with an unusual or colorful past Clive and Joan Evans and their family moved here from Hong Kong where Clive had been for many years a senior superintendent in the Hong Kong police.   They have opened their home to guests, offering five comfortable bedrooms that share a large upstairs bathroom and a downstairs toilet.   Joan is kept busy running the house and offering her guests, not only delicious breakfasts and dinners (using fresh vegetables picked from the garden), but seafood lunches served farmhouse-style round the kitchen table.   The Evans have several horses and, if you book in advance, arrangements can be made to go riding.   Bruckless House is an ideal place to stay for visiting Glencolumbkille Folk Museum, a collection of thatched Donegal farmhouses where you learn an appreciation for the hardy lives that the local people led.   From Donegal take the N56 towards Killybegs.   Bruckless House is on the right in the village of Bruckless.

BRUCKLESS HOUSE
Owners: Clive & Joan Evans
Bruckless
Co Donegal
tel: (073) 37071
5 bedrooms sharing 1 1/2 bathrooms
£13 per person B & B
Open: April to September
Credit cards: none
Farmhouse

A hundred years ago there were many grand Victorian homes in Cahersiveen, on the Kerry peninsula, but today Mount Rivers is the only one remaining. Derrick McKenna's grandfather built the house and furnished it in the grand Victorian style as befitted his status as the area's doctor. The years have been kind to Derek's family home - the gracious furniture, elegant silver and grand crystal remain as do the original fireplaces and light fixtures. The addition of modern bathrooms tucked into the corners of most of the bedrooms is the only obvious 20th-century modification. Like the sitting and the dining room, the bedrooms are filled with lovely old Victorian furniture. Everywhere I looked, displays of Victoriana cluttered the sideboards and mantleshelves. Mount Rivers is a perfect place to stay to soak up the beauties of the Ring of Kerry. An especially exciting trip is to visit the island of Skellig Michael, a craggy rock topped by an ancient monastery reached by climbing a winding stone staircase - arrangements can be made on arrival in Cahersiveen. The day trip operates only in clear, calm weather. Cahersiveen is 40 miles from Kenmare and 30 miles from Tralee on the Ring of Kerry.

MOUNT RIVERS
Owners: Derrick & Noreen McKenna
Cahersiveen
Ring of Kerry
Co Kerry
tel: (0667) 2509
6 bedrooms, 4 with private bathrooms
From £10 to £12 per person B & B
Open: Easter to October
Credit cards: none
Country home

The Londonderry Arms was built in 1848 as a coaching inn by the Marchioness of Londonderry. Her great-grandson, Sir Winston Churchill, inherited it in 1921. Frank and Moira O'Neill bought the hotel in 1947 and more recently their son Frank Junior has taken over the operation of this delightful seaside hostelry. Frank takes great care to keep an olde-worlde atmosphere in all the public rooms - bottle glass windows and dark carved furniture offer a club-like feel to the dining room. Guests gather in the back lounge for tea and scones or retire to the front sitting room to read. Upstairs the bedrooms are attractively, though plainly, decorated - those at the front have a more spacious feel to them with views of the town and the sea. One of the back bedrooms has Oriental-style antique furniture. Around you the scenic Antrim coast is full of cliffs, headlands and a succession of stunning views. You can detour into one of the Glens of Antrim where the mountains run inland parallel to each other and the world-famous Giant's Causeway is an hour's drive away. Carnlough is 35 miles north of Belfast. If you are arriving from County Donegal take the A2 to Coleraine, the A26 to Ballymena and the A42 to Carnlough.

LONDONDERRY ARMS
Owner: Frank O'Neill
Carnlough
Co Antrim BT44 0EU
tel: (0574) 85255
15 bedrooms with private bathrooms
From £17.00 to £19.50 per person B&B
Open: all year
Credit cards: all major
Family hotel

This is one of those welcoming places that guests return to time and time again - one couple is scheduled for their nineteenth visit to this lovely home. A profusion of wildflower arrangements graces the hall, dining and sitting rooms and their smell blends with that of the furniture polish used to keep the lovely old furniture gleaming bright. A hearty farmhouse dinner is served round the large dining room table - the vegetables, fruits, lamb and beef are fresh from the farm and carefully cooked by Agnes Harrington. Upstairs three of the bedrooms have en-suite bathrooms - one, a family room, has two lovely old brass and iron beds. The other three bedrooms share two bathrooms upstairs and a third downstairs. There are lots of places to go and things to see in the area - in Carrick on Shannon you can rent a cabin cruiser and meander along the River Shannon and her lakes, stopping off to visit the villages and their pubs along the way. Glencarne House is on the N4, Dublin to Sligo road, betweeen Carrick on Shannon and Boyle.

GLENCARNE HOUSE
Owner: Agnes Harrington
Carrick on Shannon
Co Roscommon
tel: (097) 67031
6 bedrooms, 3 with private bath
£10 per person B & B
Open: March to October
Credit cards: none
Farmhouse

The setting for Cashel House is impressive: at the head of Cashel Bay with Cashel Hill standing guard behind, a solid white house nestles amongst acres and acres of woodland and gardens of exotic flowering shrubs from all over the world.   Miles of garden footpaths are yours to wander and the beautiful seashore is yours to explore.   This is not the kind of hotel to spend just a night in - once you have settled into your lovely room and sampled the exquisite food, you will be glad that you have made Cashel House the base for your Connemara explorations. Graceful antiques, turf fires and lovely arrangements of freshly picked flowers create a warm country house welcome.   It feels particularly decadent to have breakfast served to you in bed on a prettily decorated tray.   All of the bedrooms are beautifully furnished and decorated.   Nine suites occupy a more modern wing and enjoy comfortable sitting areas overlooking the garden.   Tennis rackets are available so keen tennis players can enjoy the court.   To find Cashel House take the N59 from Galway (towards Clifden) through Oughterard and turn left to the village of Cashel 1 mile after Recess.   The hotel is on the shore just after the church.

CASHEL HOUSE HOTEL
Owners: Dermot & Kay McEvilly
Cashel, Connemara
Co Galway
tel: (095) 31001 telex: 50812
32 bedrooms with private bathrooms
From £39 single to £85 double
Open: March to October
Credit cards: all major
U.S. Rep: Robert Reid
Rep tel: 800-223-6510
Country house

Cashel Palace was built as the sumptuous home of the Bishop of Cashel in 1730. The bishop chose a prime location with an unparalleled view of the Rock of Cashel rising above the town topped by the ruins of a 13th-century cathedral. A grand staircase leads to the second-floor bedrooms where a lavish array of accommodation is offered: the grand Bishop's Bedroom and the Bunny Room with its whimsical Peter Rabbit frieze on the bathroom walls stand out as particular favorites. A narrow flight of stairs reaches up to the third floor where the twin-bedded rooms are much smaller in size and very country-cozy in feel, with small windows that overlook either the town or the gardens. If you desire a standard double-bedded room there are three on the ground floor. The Four Seasons Restaurant offers the opportunity for gracious dining while the Bishop's Buttery, in the old palace cellars, provides a more casual alternative. The staff are particularly friendly. One guest loves the place so much that she has been in residence for over 16 years. The palace is right in the centre of town, a perfect spot for browsing around the shops. If you expect to find the Atlantic Ocean at your doorstep you have come to the wrong Cashel - this one is northeast of Cork.

CASHEL PALACE
Owner: Ray Carroll
Cashel
Co Tipperary
tel: (062) 61411 telex: 26938
19 bedrooms with private bathrooms
From £71.50 single to £143 double
Open: all year
Credit cards: all major
U.S. Rep: Robert Reid
Rep tel: 800-223-6510
Country house

Parkstown House is 7 miles north of Cashel at Horse and Jockey - a pub and a cluster of houses on the Cork to Dublin road. This elegant old home is full of grand antiques and everything is in tiptop condition. There is no air of faded glory to Parkstown House - the wooden floors gleam and the furniture is so highly polished it reflects the lovely displays of Waterford crystal and family silver. A large master bedroom interconnects with a smaller twin bedded room that has a large bathroom. The remaining three bedrooms share the facilites of a large bathroom. Ena Maher finds that once guests have discovered her home they often go no farther, making it their base for explorations down to Waterford and the Knockmealdown mountains and up to Loch Derg. The nearby Horse and Jockey restaurant is a very pleasant place to dine but if you want to splurge you will do no better than the Four Seasons Restaurant in the Cashel Palace Hotel. The gentle lowing of the cows ambling up to the dairy every morning and evening are the only sounds that punctuate the pastoral tranquility of Parkstown House.

PARKSTOWN HOUSE
Owners: Joe & Ena Maher
Horse & Jockey
near Cashel
Co Tipperary
tel: (0504) 44315
5 bedrooms, 1 with private bathroom
From £11.50 to £12.50 per person B & B
Open: April to September
Credit cards: none
Country house

After several years of cooking abroad, John Doyle returned to his own village to remodel the village school and open it principally as a restaurant, but with four bedrooms neatly tucked under the eaves to accommodate overnight guests.   Four additional bedrooms are planned in an adjacent house.   Those in the schoolhouse, reached by means of a narrow spiral staircase, all have antique beds and one is large enough to accommodate a sofa, table and chairs.   John prepares very nice food.   A typical dinner might consist of avocado and prawn salad, homemade soup, outstandingly good steak with pepper sauce, and walnut and almond gateau. Castledermot is off the main tourist path, an interesting historic village with its round tower, Celtic crosses and the remains of Saint John's Friary across the road from the schoolhouse.   In 1967 a Viking stone known as a hogback was unearthed, the only known one in Ireland.   Doyle's Schoolhouse is located on the N9 (Dublin to Kilkenny road) 50 miles south of Dublin.

DOYLE'S SCHOOLHOUSE
Owner: John Doyle
Main Street
Castledermot
Co Kildare
tel: (0503) 44282
8 bedrooms with private bathrooms
£15 per person B & B
Open: all year
Credit cards: all major
Restaurant with rooms

Families stopping at Lisnamandra on their way north have been known to get no farther, contenting themselves with whiling away the hours in this peaceful spot and enjoying the warm farmhouse hospitality that Bert and Iris Neill offer.   Downstairs the dining and sitting rooms are large and comfortable with high ceilings.   Upstairs the bedrooms are prettily papered and decorated.   A large chest in the upstairs hallway contains extra pillows, blankets and towels and guests are encouraged to help themselves to additional supplies.   Iris offers a traditional four course farmhouse dinner and breakfast from a menu that includes yogurt, apple pancakes, grilled kippers, cheese and mushroom quiche and French toast as alternatives to the traditional Irish breakfast.   Lisnamandra is a 10-minute drive from Lough Oughter, a vast complex of lakes and rivers that delights championship and amateur fishermen with good catches of bream and roach.   Even if you don't fish Lisnamandra is a delightful place to visit for warm farmhouse hospitality, good home cooking and countryside tranquility.   Tours can be taken of the nearby Cavan crystal factory.   Lisnamandra farmhouse is 5 miles south of Cavan on the L15 (R198), 1 mile before you reach the village of Crossdoney.

LISNAMANDRA
Owners: Bert & Iris Neill
Crossdoney
Cavan
Co Cavan
tel: (049) 37196
6 bedrooms, 2 with private bathrooms
£9.75 per person B & B
Open: April to September
Credit cards: none
Farmhouse

Rock Glen Country House is a cozy hotel converted from an 18th-century hunting lodge with all the outdoor beauties of Connemara at its doorstep. Enjoy the beauties of the area, safe in the certainty that a warm welcome, superlative food and a snug retreat await you on your return to Rock Glen. An inviting grouping of plump chairs around a turf fire, the chatter of locals and guests and the warmth of the adjacent sunlounge invite you to linger in the bar. The dining room, decked out in shades of peach and pink, its tables laid with silver, complements the fine cuisine cooked by John Roche who trained as a chef in the prestigious Ashford Castle. Evangeline also worked at Ashford and it is here that they have put to work their professional training - creating an intimate countryside hotel that recalls the pleasures of a leisurely and more sedate way of life. The small comfortable bedrooms are uniform in size, decorated in pastel shades and plainly furnished, the beds covered with handwoven Irish bedspreads. Quite the nicest room is 35, a two-bedroom suite with a spacious sitting area and private balcony overlooking the sea. Take the N59 from Galway to Clifden, just after passing the church turn left towards Ballyconeely, and Rock Glen is to your right about half a mile from town.

ROCK GLEN COUNTRY HOUSE
Owners: John & Evangeline Roche
Clifden, Connemara
Co Galway
tel: (095) 21035 telex: 50915
30 bedrooms with private bathrooms
From £25 single to £67.50 double
Open: April to October
Credit cards: all major
U.S. Rep: R.S.I.
Rep tel: 800-223-1588
Country house hotel

Rose Cottage was completely remodeled in 1986 to provide simple bed and breakfast accommodation for visitors to this most lovely area. The heart of the cottage with its flagstone floors and whitewashed walls remains as the reception and dining room. Four bedrooms, each with private bathroom, have been added to one side while upstairs the roof has been raised and two larger bedrooms have been added under the eaves. The decor throughout is very plain but the warm Irish welcome and concern that guests enjoy their stay are ever present. Guests frequently stay for a week and Mary always sends them a list of the kind of food she cooks for dinner. Rose Cottage was built in the 1800s by the British who sought to establish a Quaker village at Rockfield. The local curates refused to let the cottages be occupied by Protestants in this staunchly Catholic area, so they stood empty until taken over by the Free Irish government in 1917. They sold them for £50 to Irish emigrants returning from Australia and Canada. Joe and Mary O'Toole inherited the cottage many years ago and continued to make mortgage payments to the government - 12 shillings (less than $1) twice a year. From Galway take the N59 to Clifden, turn right at the church, towards Letterfrack, for the 6-mile drive to Rockfield and Rose Cottage.

ROSE COTTAGE
Owner: Mary O'Toole
Rockfield
Moyard near Clifden
Co Galway
tel: (095) 41082
6 bedrooms with private bathrooms
£10 per person B & B
Open: Easter to September
Credit cards: none
Farmhouse

Blackheath House was built as a rectory in 1795, its most famous incumbent being the Reverend Alexander whose wife Cecile wrote many famous hymns including "There is a Green Hill Far Away", "All Things Bright and Beautiful" and "Once in Royal David's City". Joe and Margaret Erwin returned to Ireland in 1978 to convert Margaret's family home into a country house hotel and restaurant. The drawing room offers a lovely collection of family furniture and a grand piano. Guests dine downstairs in the cellar restaurant, MacDuff's, where a comfortable bistro style atmosphere prevails and dining is a la carte. Margaret puts a great deal of care into the cooking. Dining is at a leisurely pace and the service most attentive. Upstairs the bedrooms are stylishly decorated and furnished with antiques - all equipped with color televisions and modern bathrooms. If you are arriving in Northern Ireland from County Donegal take the N13 from Letterkenny to Derry. Cross the Foyle Bridge and at Limavady, take the A37 towards Coleraine and turn right on the A29 (Garvagh and Cookstown) for 4 miles and then turn right on a small road (Mascosquin) and Blackheath House is on your right.

BLACKHEATH HOUSE
Owners: Joseph & Margaret Erwin
112 Killeague Road
Blackhill nr Coleraine
Co Londonderry, BT51 4HN
tel: (026585) 433
5 bedrooms with private bathrooms
From £25 single to £40 double
Open: all year
Credit cards: VS
U.S. Rep: Robert Reid
Rep tel: 800-223-6510
Country house

It is worth visiting Northern Ireland just to stay here. The house is lovingly decorated, with gracious antiques and bouquets of fresh garden flowers adding the finishing touches. Our bedroom (overlooking an immaculate garden) had more comforts than many four star hotels: sightseeing information; a tray set with teapot, kettle, teabags, coffee and chocolate and even a little box of After Eight Mints by the bedside. Plump comforters top the beds, fluffy towels hang on the old-fashioned towel rail - all coordinating in shades of pink with the curtains and the carpet. In addition two bedrooms have small bathrooms with showers neatly built into the rooms. All this and wonderful farmhouse food as well - five courses of it beautifully cooked, served and presented. Be warned: do not overindulge in the first four courses as the dessert trolley offers such tempting desserts that they are impossible to resist. The end of the day is celebrated with a cup of tea and cakes with Elizabeth and James around the drawing room fire. It goes without saying that you should plan on staying here for several days. If you are arriving from County Donegal follow the same driving directions as for Blackheath House but continue along the A29 for 7 miles turning left on the B66 towards Ballymoney - the house is on the right.

GREENHILL HOUSE
Owners: James & Elizabeth Hegarty
24 Greenhill Road
Aghadowey nr Coleraine
Co Londonderry, BT51 4EU
tel: (026 585) 241
7 bedrooms, 2 with private bathrooms
From £10.50 to £11.50 per person B & B
Open: March to October
Credit cards: none
Farmhouse

Ashford Castle was built over a period of 30 years by Lord Ardilaun in the 19th century. Incorporated into its castellated facade are the remains of the 13th-century de Burgo Castle and the original Ashford House, built in the style of a French chateau. This certainly was a sumptuous residence and in more recent years Ashford has been renovated and luxuriously appointed to create one of Europe's premier castle hotels. The decor of the public rooms is lavish and opulent, the views across the lake stunning. This is a hotel that attracts kings and presidents - the billiard room was built for King Edward VII when he came to stay in 1905; for President Reagan's visit in 1984 a luxurious bed was commissioned. After a splendid dinner in one of the castle's two restaurants, you can enjoy Irish entertainment in the Dungeon Bar, take a stroll through the lakeside gardens or saunter into the adjacent village of Cong. The setting on the shores of beautiful Lough Corrib with its hundreds of islands, bays and coves is stunning. A nine-hole golf course and tennis courts are reserved for guests' use. The Lough is famous for its fishing and shooting for duck, pheasant, snipe and woodcock can be arranged. The castle is 27 miles north of Galway on the shores of Lough Corrib.

ASHFORD CASTLE
Manager: Rory Murphy
Cong
Co Mayo
tel: (091) 46003
84 bedrooms with private bathrooms
From £60 single to £160 double
Open: all year
Credit cards: all major
U.S. Rep: Ashford Castle
Rep tel: 800-346-7007
Castle hotel

Declan and Michael Ryan have gained quite a reputation for their food over the last decade: Michelin has consistently awarded them a star rating and they are recommended in many food guides.   They are proud of being among the first Irish restaurants to promote the use of fresh, local produce (nothing bar the wine comes from more than 5 miles away) and cheese - as Declan explained to me, it is only in the last decade that the Irish have realized that they can produce cheese as good as any in Europe.   They offer a short a la carte menu, an extensive tasting menu and a set dinner every evening except Sunday.   Connoisseurs will appreciate some rare wines featured on the extensive wine list.   While this is very much a city establishment within easy walking distance of the town, the Victorian building is surrounded by trees, giving it a country house feel.   The newly remodeled bedrooms are full of 20th-century gadgets; a remote control TV, bedside radio and telephone to name but a few.   (Several rooms are still in the process of being remodeled.)   This is one of the few hotels that you can easily reach by train - the station is a 2-minute taxi ride away.   The hotel is located just off the N8, the main Waterford to Cork road.   As you enter the city of Cork, watch for a signpost to your right just after the first roundabout on the city outskirts.   Follow the narrow road up the hill and down again: Arbutus Lodge is on your left.

ARBUTUS LODGE
Owners: The Ryan Family
Cork
Co Cork
tel: (021) 51237
20 bedrooms with private bathrooms
From £36.50 single to £98 double
Open: all year
Credit cards: all major
City hotel

I really wanted to include a farmhouse that would provide a stepping-off point for those arriving at Shannon Airport and heading north.   I visited many in this area and decided after deliberation that there were none better than that at which I stayed: Fergus View.   Mary Kelleher was able to provide, with just a half hour's notice, one of the tastiest farmhouse meals - piping hot soup, roast beef accompanied by a multitude of home-grown vegetables and a cream caramel for dessert.   The small residents' lounge has lots of information on the local area. The nearby Burren with its lunar-like landscape and distinctive flora is most interesting, the magnificent Cliffs of Moher are nearby and Bunratty Castle and Folk Park are less than an hour's drive away.   The bedrooms are freshly decorated and warmly heated but very small in size.   One has the advantage of an en-suite bathroom while the remaining rooms share two bathrooms.   Shannon Airport lies 23 miles to the south.   From the airport take the N18 to Ennis, the N85 towards Lisdoonvarna, turn first right to Corofin and after passing through the village the farmhouse is on your left after about two miles.

FERGUS VIEW
Owner: Mary Kelleher
Kilnaboy
Corofin
Co Clare
tel: (065) 27606
6 bedrooms, 1 with private bathroom
£10 per person B & B
Open: mid-March to September
Credit cards: none
Farmhouse

Enniscoe House is owned and run by Susan Kellett, a descendant of the original family who settled here in the 1670s. This is the home of Susan and her young son, and staying as her guest gives you a glimpse of what it was like to live in a grand country mansion - the old family furniture, portraits, books and family memorabilia are yours to enjoy. The lofty rooms are decorated true to the Georgian period. The three front bedrooms are of enormous proportions, reached by a grand elliptical staircase. Those in the older part of the house are small by comparison yet still very nice. Susan has her hands full just keeping up on the maintenance yet she has found time to involve herself in the local historical society which assists those of Irish extraction in tracing their County Mayo ancestors. As if this was not enough, somehow Susan finds time for the cooking, offering her guests the very best of country house food. Fishermen, or would-be fishermen, can borrow rods and try their hand at fishing in the adjacent Lough Conn. Boats and ghillies are available for hire. There is also a self-catering cottage in the grounds, which, though modernized, still retains its old fireplace. From Ballina go to Crossmolina, turn left in the town for Castlebar and the house is on your left 2 miles out of town.

ENNISCOE HOUSE
Owner: Susan Kellett
Castlehill near Crossmolina
Co Mayo
tel: (096) 31112 telex: 40855
6 bedrooms, 5 with private bathrooms
From £38 single to £60 double
Open: April to September
Credit cards: all major
U.S. Rep: Robert Reid
Rep tel: 800-223-6510
Country house hotel

Joe Moffatt was born at Kilmurray House but after his father's death the family abandoned the farm and emigrated to England. Joe always dreamed of his home in Ireland and many years later he returned with his young bride, Madge, to claim his farm. The house was derelict and their first thought was to build a modern bungalow nearby, but thankfully they realized the potential in Kilmurray House and persevered in its restoration. When their home was complete, Madge decided to open it to guests. The bedrooms are very nicely decorated in bright colors with coordinating bedspreads and walls - five have private bathrooms and the sixth a bathroom across the hall. The downstairs bedroom is suitable for wheelchair access and plans are under way to equip its bathroom for disabled persons. The dining room tables are set with checked cloths and Madge discusses with her guests what they would like to eat for dinner - all the vegetables, fruit, beef and lamb are from the farm. Joe is active in the local fishing club and enjoys planning outings for the avid fishermen who come to these parts. Not surprisingly, Madge won the Irish "Farmhouse of the Year" competition in 1984. From Ballina go to Crossmolina, turn left in the town for Castlebar, pass the gates of Enniscoe House and take the first turn to your right for the 2-mile drive to the farm.

KILMURRAY HOUSE
Owner: Madge Moffatt
Castlehill
Crossmolina
Co Mayo
tel: (096) 31227
6 bedrooms, 5 with private bathrooms
£10 per person B & B
Open: March to October
Credit cards: none
Farmhouse

Cleevaun has the advantage of being purpose-built as a bed and breakfast so each of the bedrooms has a modern en-suite bathroom. The weather was blustery and cool when we stayed, but inside efficient central heating kept the house toasty and we appreciated the abundance of hot water in the shower and the luxury of warm towels hot from the heated towel rail. The furniture in all the bedrooms is light modern pine, the decor tasteful and uncluttered, and several rooms have lovely views over the fields to the mouth of Dingle Bay. The very nicest touch is the note that Ursula Sheehy leaves in each of her guestrooms inviting guests to the lounge for a cup of tea or coffee and to browse through books "which will help you appreciate the beauty and folklore of the area. It would be a pity to have come so far and not experience the peace and tranquility which the unspoiled scenery of this area has to offer". Tommy and Ursula provide their guests with lots of information on where to dine in nearby Dingle and in the morning offer the choice of a traditional Irish breakfast, cheese and fresh fruit or hot crumpets and syrup with bran muffins. Children are very welcome and there is a large garden with play equipment. Cleevaun is 1 mile out of Dingle on the road to Slea Head.

CLEEVAUN
Owners: Tommy & Ursula Sheehy
Lady's Cross
Dingle
Co Kerry
tel: (066) 51108
5 bedrooms with private bathrooms
£10 per person B & B
Open: March to October
Credit cards: none
Bed & Breakfast

Doyle's Seafood Bar is famous the world over for excellent seafood. A small village shop and pub built in 1790 house the famous bar with its flagstone floor and cozy arrangements of tables and chairs. The acquisition of the house next door means that now John and Stella can offer overnight accommodation as well as fine dining. The two houses are interconnected yet self-contained, so that guests can come and go to the bar and restaurant but will not have their peace disturbed when they are trying to sleep. The eight guestrooms have private bathrooms and are decorated in a style appropriate to the cozy cottage they occupy - dainty pieces of Victorian furniture collected over the years add charming touches. Dingle is a 2 1/2-hour drive from Limerick and anyone in the town can quickly direct you to Doyle's though finding street parking in this busy little town may prove a problem.

DOYLE'S SEAFOOD BAR & TOWNHOUSE
Owners: John & Stella Doyle
John Street
Dingle
Co Kerry
tel: (066) 51174
8 bedrooms with private bathrooms
From £22 to £24.50 per person B & B
Open: mid-March to mid-November
Credit cards: all major
Restaurant with rooms

Set in the heart of Yeats country, this charming hotel is impeccably run by Andrew and Barbara Greenstein, Americans who have made Drumlease Glebe House their home.   And what a beautiful home it is - the pine floors are topped by Oriental carpets, European antiques decorate the rooms, fine paintings grace the walls and masses of flowers add a homey touch.   Andy and Barbara create a convivial house party, chatting with guests before dinner, helping in the dining room and retiring with them for coffee and conversation into the drawing room.   The food is outstanding, beautifully presented and thoughtfully served on polished tables laid with silver and Waterford crystal - the soft glow of candlelight completes the romantic scene.   (There are no choices but Barbara discusses the evening meal with guests in the morning.)   Wellies are provided for those who wish to tramp around the grounds - the dogs Coalie and Poteen love to accompany visitors.   The idyllic country scene is completed by Joyce, Yeats and O'Casey, the donkeys, in the field next to the swimming pool.   From Dublin take the N4 to within 2 miles of Sligo and turn right to Dromahair.   Just before the village (10 miles) turn right and the house is on your right after 2 miles.   (The house is unsuitable for children.)

DRUMLEASE GLEBE HOUSE
Owners: Andrew & Barbara Greenstein
Dromahair near Sligo
Co Leitrim
tel: (071) 64141
7 bedrooms with private bathrooms
From £29 single to £66 double
Open: April to September
Credit cards: AX, MC, VS
U.S. Rep: Robert Reid
Rep tel: 800-223-6510
Country house

The Stanford Village Inn is a traditional Irish country pub that offers accommodation. This rural bar was opened over a hundred years ago by Della McGowan's great grandfather and remains today much as it always has been - not much to look at on the outside but warm and cozy on the inside, filled with locals, the bottles stacked on ceiling-high shelves, brass lanterns hung from the ceiling, guitars and a fiddle at the ready for impromptu music making. Della showed me her grandfather's fiddle and recounted tales of how he used to play while the village children danced and, she added wryly, her grandmother did all of the work. The pub has been extended into an adjacent building but the same snug feel has been kept, with exposed stone walls, tweed curtains and old rafters hung with brass beer taps. The simple, yet attractive, restaurant overlooks the garden and offers a set dinner. Upstairs, well away from the noise of the bar, are five modern comfortable bedrooms all of which have showers and share two bathrooms. To find this traditional hostelry take the N4 to within 2 miles of Sligo. The turn to Dromahair is to your right. Drive into the village (10 miles) and Stanford Village Inn is on your right. From Sligo follow the N16 towards Manorhamilton and you see signs for Dromahair just as you leave the town.

STANFORD VILLAGE INN
Owners: Tom & Della McGowan
Dromahair near Sligo
Co Leitrim
tel: (071) 64140
5 bedrooms sharing 2 bathrooms
£12 per person B & B
Open: all year
Credit cards: none
Village inn

Helen Kirrane works very hard to ensure that her house is picture-perfect: guests praise its pretty decor and return here to make it their home away from home in Dublin. The sitting room was the most elegant I saw in a guesthouse, with its soft pastel Chinese silk carpet and exquisite antique furniture. The adjacent dining room table was set for what Helen terms her breakfast celebration when she serves home-baked cakes and pies, yogurt and fish as well as the traditional Irish breakfast. Upstairs the bedrooms are individually decorated in soft pastels. Those at the front are soundproofed to ensure a quiet night's sleep while those at the back have delightful views across the garden and cricket ground to the river bank. All rooms have direct dial phones, color televisions and bathrooms with showers. There is parking for cars in front and the 63 and 84 buses leave nearby for the 2-mile ride into the city. Anglesea Townhouse is located in the Ballsbridge suburb of Dublin near the American Embassy.

ANGLESEA TOWNHOUSE
Owner: Sean & Helen Kirrane
63 Anglesea Road
Ballsbridge
Dublin 4
tel: (01) 683877 telex: 91475
7 bedrooms with private bathrooms
£22 per person B & B
Open: all year
Credit cards: VS
Guesthouse

Michael O'Brien, the friendly owner of Ariel House, offers a warm Irish welcome to his guesthouse. Michael returned to Ireland in the 60s, after working in hotels in San Francisco and London, to convert his family home into a guesthouse. The bedrooms are modest with fitted unit furniture and simple decoration - nine have baths and six have showers. The plain decor is far more suited to the rooms in the 1960s style addition that overlooks the garden than those in the main house which have towering 15-foot ceilings. All are equipped with color televisions, phones and hairdryers. For a room with charm splurge and reserve room 27, a spacious suite with a large picture window framing the garden - with its small sofa, antique table and chairs and large bathroom resplendent with whirlpool tub it is well worth the additional 50% tariff. The dining room extends into a conservatory and is most attractively decorated with groups of Victorian tables and chairs - Marion, the chef, prepares a delightful five course dinner every evening except Saturday. There is ample off-street parking. Ariel House is located on a quiet suburban street, 2 miles from the heart of Dublin. Just down the road are Jury's and the Berkley Court hotels and it is an easy walk to the 5, 6, 7 and 7A bus routes and the DART (Dublin Area Rapid Transit).

ARIEL HOUSE
Owner: Michael O'Brien
52 Lansdowne Road
Ballsbridge
Dublin 4
tel: (01) 685512
15 bedrooms
From £38.50 single to £55 double
Closed: December 20th to January 1st
Credit cards: AX, MC, VS
Guesthouse

The location is absolutely perfect - just off St Stephen's Green in the heart of Georgian Dublin. As its name suggests, the house stands as a tall narrow, four-story, Georgian townhouse. While the house is over 200 years old, everything has been restored and renovated adding light and freshness. Up the tall narrow staircase the 10 bedrooms each have small bathrooms with showers neatly tucked into the corner. All are decorated in soft pastels accented with pretty patterned drapes, furnished with light pine furniture and equipped with television and radio. If you have difficulty with stairs, or large unwieldy suitcases, you may want to request one of the bedrooms on the lower floors. A snug lounge occupies the front room of the house on the ground floor. Accessed by a narrow flight of winding stairs, the old basement is now a small comfortable restaurant, The Ante Room, where guests are served their breakfast. The lunch and dinner menus offer Irish ingredients cooked in the popular French style. The garden is now a secure carpark where guests can store their cars for the duration of their stay and set out to explore this interesting city on foot, returning home to rest and recuperate whenever they are tired.

GEORGIAN HOUSE GUEST HOUSE
Owner: Annette O'Sullivan
20 Lower Baggot Street
Dublin 2
tel: (01) 604300
10 bedrooms with private bathrooms
From £25 to £32 per person B & B
Open: all year
Credit cards: all major
Guesthouse

Just a five-minute walk from St Stephen's Green, within easy walking distance of all the sights and shops of Dublin, Kilronan House offers visitors a warm welcome. Everything is in apple pie order, from the gleaming brasses on the front door to the fresh paintwork in the bedrooms. Public rooms consist of a comfortable lounge and a breakfast room (dinner is served only between October and Easter). Up the narrow winding staircase the design of the bedrooms has been well thought out - small bathrooms are tucked into the corner of all but three rooms (these three have showers and washbasins and share toilets down the hall) and fitted furniture is combined with antique pieces. All the bedrooms have excellent reading lights, telephones, tea making facilites and hairdryers. If you have difficulty with stairs, request one of the lower floor rooms. Parking is on the street in front of the house.

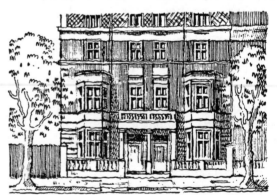

KILRONAN HOUSE
Owner: Josephine Murray
70 Adelaide Road
Dublin 2
tel: (01) 755266/751562
11 bedrooms, 8 with private bathrooms
From £28 single to £42 double
Closed: December 23rd to January 1st
Credit cards: none
Guesthouse

I visited the Russell Court Hotel during the second week it was open and found it to be quite the nicest small hotel in Dublin. I was shown around by a most enthusiastic manager who assured me that the Russell Court's aim was to become a small personable hotel where guests have a name not a room number. However, when I telephoned several months later I found that the management had changed, so now I hope that the hotel is living up to its former ideals and the promise that the fashionable decor offers. Just a few steps from St Stephen's Green, the Russell Court Hotel has a perfect location for exploring Dublin on foot. (In fact a car is a handicap as the hotel has no car park and on-street parking is metered.) The decor throughout is stylish modern, very reminscent in many aspects of Art Deco. Contemporary black leather sofas and chairs adorn the lounge and along with the laquered black tables provide a sharp contrast to the pastel paintwork. The adjacent Mucky Duck Bar with its duck caricatures and large papier mache mother and father ducks brings a smile to your face and promises a convivial, lively atmosphere. The small restaurant offers French cuisine. Bedrooms have a very freshly tailored, unfussy feel to them and soundproofing blocks out traffic noise. The prices are very reasonable for a fashionably decorated hotel in a prime location.

RUSSELL COURT HOTEL
Manager: Una Hanly
Harcourt Street
Dublin 2
tel: (01) 784066/784841
22 bedrooms with private bathrooms
From £51 single to £68 double
Open: all year
Credit cards: AX, MC, VS
Small city hotel

Just as we were about to go to press with a reprint of "Irish Country Inns" I received a letter from Ann O'Dwyer announcing that she and her son Michael had bought this attractive guesthouse in the Rathgar suburb of Dublin. She assures me that like St Aiden's previous owner she too loves to have guests in her home and takes great pains to give them lots of advice on the sights and restaurants of Dublin. This is one of those places where guests linger, chatting in the dining room or gathered in the comfortable lounge surrounded by books and games and Victoriana. The bedrooms are all charmingly decorated with Laura Ashley sprigged wallpapers with matching bedspreads and curtains. Several of the rooms are large enough to accommodate families or alternately children can have their own snug single room. The rooms vary in size from large, high-ceiling rooms to smaller, square rooms in the more modern extension to snug attic rooms tucked under the eaves of the old house. Brighton Road is a quiet suburban street a short walk from the 15A, 15B and 15C bus routes that take you the 2 miles to the city centre. If you have a car, off-road parking is provided at the rear of the house.

ST AIDEN'S GUESTHOUSE
Owner: Ann O'Dwyer
32 Brighton Road
Rathgar
Dublin 6
tel: (01) 902011
14 bedrooms, 7 with private bathrooms
£17 per person B & B
Open: all year
Credit cards: AX, MC, VS
Guesthouse

The Irish nobility and country gentlemen needed to spend time in Dublin, so in 1824 the Shelbourne opened its doors to the gentry who did not have a residence in the city.   Since day one the Shelbourne has been "the" place to stay and today it remains as Dublin's deluxe hotel, suffused with the elegance of other eras.   The comings and goings of Dublin are reflected in the enormous gilt mirrors of the Lord Mayor's Lounge.   Traditional decor, good conversation and the presence of Dublin characters combine to make the Horseshoe Bar a most convivial place. The very elegant Aisling restaurant provides equally elegant food, while the adjacent Causerie grill room provides a less sophisticated dining alternative.   The bedrooms and opulent suites have been recently refurbished to the highest of standards.   (The Executive wing has quite a different boxy, modern hotel-like character to it, but these rooms are primarily allocated to single business clients.) This landmark historic hotel overlooks St Stephen's Green, a refreshing oasis of greenery in the centre of this bustling city.

SHELBOURNE HOTEL
Manager: Gerald Lawless
St Stephen's Green
Dublin 2
tel: (01) 766471 telex: 93653
170 bedrooms with private bathrooms
From £105 single to £180 double
Open: all year
Credit cards: all major
U.S. Rep: Trusthouse Forte
Rep tel: 800-223-5672
City hotel

Sitting in the peaceful Priory Lodge garden, it is hard to imagine that the city of Dublin is just 20 minutes away. This really is the place to stay if you want to visit Dublin during the day and retire to country home style accommodation in a quiet suburb at night. Dermot Long served for many years as the private secretary and chef for a wealthy Irish industrialist who preferred to entertain at his many homes than endure staying in impersonal hotels. When he died, Dermot decided to establish the kind of home away from home that his fomer employer would have approved of - and thus was born the idea for Priory Lodge. Dermot does all the cooking and, besides breakfast, offers his guests a four course evening meal accompanied by a short wine list. Antiques and plump cushioned chairs make the lounge a most inviting place. The three large upstairs bedrooms have adjoining dressing areas and en-suite bathrooms. The two smaller downstairs bedrooms share a bathroom. Priory Lodge is in a south Dublin suburb, very convenient for the Dun Laoghaire ferry. If arriving from the ferry, turn left in Blackrock on Mount Merrion Road and Grove Avenue is the fifth road to your left.

PRIORY LODGE
Owners: Dermot & Pauline Long
Grove Avenue
Blackrock
near Dublin
Co Dublin
tel: (01) 888221/832267
5 bedrooms, 3 with private bathrooms
From £15 to £25 per person B & B
Open: all year
Credit cards: VS
Country house

Elma Nobles finds that most of her guests have come to her farmhouse through recommendations by friends or returning guests - a sure sign of a welcoming place to stay.   The farmhouse is old but the interior has been completely modernized. A good home-cooked three course dinner is served in the dining room, then guests go their individual ways to return at 10.30pm for tea, cakes and conversation round the lounge fire.   Accommodation is offered in both ground-floor and upstairs bedrooms - all are freshly painted and four have private bathrooms.   The cows arrive every morning and evening to be milked and the antics of the local pony club, which meets in a neighboring field, are great fun to watch.   Nearby is Castlecoole, Ireland's finest classical mansion and open to the public.   A few miles farther afield is the extensive network of underground chambers that makes up the impressive Marble Arch Caves.   From Enniskillen take the B80 towards Tempo, turn first left towards Chantry Hill and Lackaboy Farmhouse is on the right after 3/4 mile.

LACKABOY FARMHOUSE
Owner: Elma Nobles
Tempo Road
Enniskillen BT74 6HR
Co Fermanagh
tel: (0365) 22488
10 bedrooms, 4 with private bathrooms
£10 to £11 per person B & B
Open: all year
Credit cards: none
Farmhouse

I sought out Smyth's Village Hotel because I had received such a nice letter of recommendation from Elizabeth and Charlie Sweeney.   I arrived at Smyth's, letter in hand, to find that the Sweeneys were in residence - back again for their eighth visit, for they - like many others - make this their home when they arrive from Shannon, rest up for a few days and return here at the end of their holiday to spend time with their friends the Smyth family.   The hotel was built in 1974 and designed as three interconnecting Irish cottages.   The Smyth family pride themselves on reflecting the simple culture and traditions of Irish village life.   Everything is simple and functional Irish country style - the Liscannor flag floors, Donegal tweed curtains (lined in the bright red woolen fabric from which Connemara girls used to make their petticoats), homespun tablemats, sugan (rope and wood) chairs, latch-key doors, blackened beam ceilings, and the roaring turf fire hung with blackened pots.   Upstairs bedrooms are more spacious than those on the ground floor, but all have private bathrooms and central heating.   From Shannon go to Sixmilebridge where you turn towards Tulla, drive through Kilmurry and Kilkishen and turn right for Feakle - the hotel is on the outskirts of the village.   The roads are small and narrow and it's easy to get lost so ask for a map when you make your reservation.

SMYTH'S VILLAGE HOTEL
Owners: The Smyth Family
Feakle
Co Clare
tel: (0609) 24002
12 bedrooms with private bathrooms
£12.65 single, £22.50 double
Open: April to October
Credit cards: none
Countryside hotel

Betty Breen offers a most congenial place to stay for visitors to this, the sunniest and driest part of Ireland. Betty takes great pride in her home and the flower filled garden that surrounds it. Guests meet each other around the dining room table in the evening when Betty serves a four course dinner - on the occasion of my last visit, fresh grilled trout and mouthwatering strawberry pie with an abundance of cream from the farm's cows were the order of the day. Betty and Tom find that many of their guests stay several days, so she can consult them about just what they would like for dinner. Upstairs the bedrooms are prettily decorated and in immaculate order: several are large family rooms and all have beautiful views of the lovely garden. In the field facing the farmhouse are the ruins of a 13th-century church and some old stones. Tom is happy to draw maps for hikers showing them where to go and what to see. Fishermen can try their luck in the River Bann that flows through the 285-acre farm. Clone House lies 2 miles southwest of the village of Ferns. From the N11 coming south take the first left after passing the church, turn first right and follow signs for the farm down the country lanes.

CLONE HOUSE
Owners: Betty & Tom Breen
Ferns
Co Wexford
tel: (054) 66113
5 bedrooms sharing 2 bathrooms
£10 per person B & B
Open: all year
Credit cards: none
Farmhouse

This welcoming farmhouse is an ideal place to stay if you intend to make a day trip to the Aran Islands. Mary will make your ferry reservations, ensure that you receive an early breakfast and that a hot dinner awaits you on your return. Run by a mother and daughter team, both called Mary, Corrib View Farm has such good food that they find that guests who often intend to stay for only one or two nights extend their visits. Daughter Mary does the cooking and very nicely so - just as you think your meal is over she presents cakes "to nibble" with your coffee. All the fruits and vegetables are fresh from the garden. The bedrooms are small and snug - one larger family room has a private bathroom while the other four rooms share two bathrooms. A fire burns brightly in the sitting room and the house is warmed by central heating. Old family furniture decorates the rooms and an atmosphere of homely friendliness prevails. Corrib View Farm is located in a peaceful country setting yet near enough to main roads to make it ideal for exploring Connemara. From Galway take the N84 (Castlebar road) for 6 miles to Clonboo Cross where the 2-mile drive to Corrib View Farm and Annaghdown are signposted to your left.

CORRIB VIEW FARM
Owners: The Scott Family
Annaghdown
Galway
Co Galway
tel: (091) 91114
5 bedrooms, 1 with private bathroom
£10 per person B & B
Open: May to September
Credit cards: none
Farmhouse

This elegant three-story Regency house, formerly the dower-house of the Courtown estate, has an atmosphere of refined elegance created by your vivacious hostess, Mary Bowe. Mary has great charm and energy - on the occasion of our stay she chatted with guests before dinner, made the rounds during dinner and was back again at breakfast checking up to make certain that everything was perfect. The house is full of antiques, classic pieces that transport you back to the days of gracious living in grand houses. Ours was an especially lovely, large, twin-bedded room with impressive, well polished furniture, elegant decor and a grand bathroom. I found the other bedrooms equally pretty. Dinner is served in the conservatory dining room and the food is a delight - superb French and Irish dishes graciously served to you in true country house style. This is one of the few hotels in Ireland where it is appropriate to dress for dinner. An atmosphere of formal luxury prevails - it is quite unsuitable for children. Marfield House is 55 miles from Dublin. Take the N11 south to Gorey, and as you enter the town turn left, before going under the railway bridge, onto the Courtown Road: the house is on your right after a mile.

MARFIELD HOUSE HOTEL
Owner: Mary Bowe
Gorey
Co Wexford
tel: (055) 21124 telex: 80757
12 bedrooms with private bathrooms
No singles, double to £110
Open: all year
Credit cards: none
U.S. Rep: Robert Reid
Rep tel: 800-223-6510
Country house

If you enjoy horse-riding, Tillman and Collette Anhold offer the experienced rider week-long riding vacations. On arrival at the farm, Collette sees that you are settled into one of the snug, pine-panelled bedrooms, then it's off to the stables to meet your fine Irish hunter. Your four-legged friend is yours to ride just when and where you want to - along miles of unspoiled beaches, through green mountain forests and along a cross-country course jumping walls and wooden fences. You are expected to look after him by feeding, grooming and tacking up. Collette provides a hearty breakfast, and a full four course dinner - serving it to guests seated around the large dining room table. A spirit of happy camaraderie prevails as guests gather in the evening around the fire in the large stone fireplace to have horsey conversations. If you wish to range farther afield, Tillman can also arrange 7- and 14-day treks where overnight accommodation is provided in traditional farmhouses. As you will not need a car for your holiday, it is suggested that you take the train to Sligo where Collette or Tillman will meet you.

HORSE HOLIDAY FARM
Owners: Tillman & Collette Anhold
Grange
Co Sligo
tel: (071) 66152
7 bedrooms with private bathrooms
£370 per person per week
* Dinner, B & B and horse*
Open: Easter to mid-October
Credit cards: none
U.S. Rep: Fran Jurga
Rep tel: 617-368-8106
Farmhouse & stables

I was welcomed to Hazel House Farm by accordian music as Matt Cunningham played traditional Irish folk music for his departing guests. It was a delightful picture, with Matt playing and sons Joseph and Eric dancing traditional Irish dances. Matt's wife, Kathleen, assures me that this is a custom of the house: whenever Matt is home he plays for guests either in the morning or after dinner - accordian, tin whistle, banjo and fiddle are his instruments. He has recorded several albums and in 1987 was invited to the United States to play for the Kennedy Family. The Cunninghams' farmhouse is a modern bungalow but the welcome and the cup of tea and scones give a delightful old-fashioned hospitality. Kathleen is happy to outline scenic drives into Conemara and to nearby Ashford Castle. The modern bedrooms are neat and tidy: five share two bathrooms and one has a bathroom en suite. If you are travelling with children, they will have the four Cunningham children as playmates. From Galway take the N84 towards Castlebar - 12 miles out of Galway the farm is signposted to your right, 1 mile off the main road in the peaceful countryside.

HAZEL HOUSE FARMHOUSE
Owners: Matt & Kathleen Cunningham
Mausrevagh
Headford
Co Galway
tel: (091) 91204
6 bedrooms, 1 with private bathroom
£10 per person B & B
Open: April to September
Credit cards: none
Farmhouse

Inishbofin is a small island off Ireland's west coast where 200 residents eke out a living farming and fishing. Overlooking the broad natural harbour, whose entrance is guarded by the ruins of a 16th-century pirate's castle, is Day's Hotel. As the name suggests, the Day family is very involved in the running of this simple family hotel: Margaret Day works hard to see that visitors enjoy their stay; son John runs the pub next door - it's a convivial place where locals gather in the evening with their instruments for music and singing; sons Kieran and Christopher return to the island to help during the summer and daughter Mary does all the cooking. Quite the nicest room is the dining room whose floor-to-ceiling windows frame views of the harbour and the rocky hills. The bedrooms are very simply decorated, clean and tidy: eight have private bathrooms and there are three additional bathrooms for the remaining bedrooms. An open fishing boat and the mail boat take visitors to and from the island and the 45-minute journey is half the fun. The boats leave from Cleggan pier at 11:30am and 6pm and return from Inishbofin at at 9am and 5pm. Be at the pier half an hour before sailing time: tickets can be bought at the Pier Bar for about £12 round trip. Sailings depend on weather conditions so it's best to phone ahead (095) 44261 and verify departure times.

DAY'S HOTEL
Owner: Margaret Day
Inishbofin Island
Co Galway
tel: (095) 45803
20 bedrooms, 8 with private bathrooms
£17 per person B & B
Open: Easter to October
Credit cards: VS
Island hotel

Assolas Country House has one of the loveliest settings in Ireland - you drive up the gravel driveway bordered by a neatly clipped hedge to the ivy-covered house with its backdrop of old trees.   In the foreground a green lawn slopes down to the river where a little wooden footbridge crosses the weir, beyond which lies a placid lake with graceful swans and gently bobbing rowing boats.   Small wonder that these delightful gardens have won the coveted National Gardens award.   This atmosphere of relaxing tranquility is continued indoors and you can be sure of a warm welcome from the Bourke family.   Bedrooms in the main house are furnished in casual country style: try one of the enormous front bedrooms overlooking the garden.   Three more modern guestrooms are adjacent to the house in the Garden Court.   Guests assemble for pre-dinner drinks in the drawing room and make their selection from the four course set dinner menu.   A choice of dishes is given for each course.   After dinner coffee is served around the fire in the drawing room and a country house party atmosphere prevails.   The best way to find Assolas Country House is from the N72, Mallow to Killarney road.   The house is signposted to your right 12 miles from Mallow - do not approach from Kanturk.

ASSOLAS COUNTRY HOUSE
Owners: The Bourke Family
Kanturk
Co Cork
tel: (029) 50015
10 bedrooms with private bathrooms
From £42 single to £98 double
Open: Easter to October
Credit cards: AX
U.S. Rep: Robert Reid
Rep tel: 800-223-6510
Country house

Dinner at Lennoxbrook is usually trout fresh from the stream, and, if you care to, you can catch it yourself (or Paul will gladly catch it for you). A choice of a red or white wine is offered with dinner and, while trout is always available, Pauline also offers pork and lamb fresh from the farm. There are lots of activities besides fishing, which are especially appealing to children: large grounds where they can romp and play, a swing on the oak tree, a dinghy to row in the stream, the donkey Mrs, a large old haybarn, hens to feed and children to play with (Paul and Pauline have two young daughters). Ancient monuments abound in the surrounding area, with Newgrange, Knowth and Dowth being the primary attractions. Besides having lots to see and do, the farmhouse is quite lovely. Beautiful family antique furniture, mementos and pictures decorate every room for Paul is the fifth generation of his family to call Lennoxbrook home. The front bedrooms are particularly prettily decorated, their small print papers complementing the lovely old furniture. Lennoxbrook is about an hour and a half's drive from Dublin Airport, making it an ideal place to stay if your destination is Donegal. The house is on the N3, Dublin to Cavan road, 3 miles beyond Kells (often labelled Ceanannas Mor on maps).

LENNOXBROOK
Owners: Paul & Pauline Mullan
Kells (Ceanannas Mor)
Co Meath
tel: (046) 45902
5 bedrooms sharing 2 bathrooms
£10 per person B & B
Open: March to November
Credit cards: none
Farmhouse

Just down the road from the Park Hotel, Hawthorne House offers visitors an immaculate guesthouse within steps of Kenmare's busy streets, yet far enough away to ensure a peaceful night's sleep.   A large car park provides safe off-road parking. Inside, the old house has received a complete facelift with light pine replacing all the old woodwork and doors, and pastel paints and soft pastel carpets giving a light, airy feel.   The bedrooms, all named after disticts around Kenmare, are very nicely decorated in a bright modern style.   Derrynid and Neidin are superior rooms, having the additional facilities of a spacious sitting area, color television, hairdryer and electric blanket.   The restaurant has a very feminine flavor, with pine chairs and tables covered with pink and white tablecloths, pink carpet and .pink velvet drapes.   Ann Browne cooks a very nice four course dinner and guests select wine from a list compiled by her husband Jerry who is head waiter at the adjacent Park Hotel.   There are lots to see and do in the area - Ann gives advice and even has printed sheets outlining six daytrips from Kenmare.   Kenmare is about a three-hour drive from Shannon, a perfect spot for touring the Ring of Kerry.

HAWTHORNE HOUSE
Owner: Ann Browne
Shelbourne Street
Kenmare
Co Kerry
tel: (064) 41035
8 bedrooms with private bathrooms
From £11 to £14 per person B & B
Closed: February
Credit cards: none
Guesthouse

The Park Hotel began life in 1897 as the Great Southern Hotel Kenmare to provide a convenient overnight stop for railway travellers en route to or from the Ring of Kerry, and has recently been restored and refurbished beyond its original grandeur. The Park has a splendid collection of interesting and very beautiful antique furniture displayed throughout the public rooms, along the wide corridors and in the elegant suites. Guests are greeted by a blazing coal fire which casts its glow towards the cozy bar and lounge and you sit down at a partners' desk to register before being shown to your room. Such touches give a small hotel feeling to this large hotel. Exquisite accommodations are provided in six very luxurious and very pricey apartments with splendid views out over the Kenmare Bay. Bedrooms in the main hotel are large and pleasant, those in the newer wing uniform in size - all with big city prices. The cooking is excellent and has been awarded a Michelin star. The menu offers some tempting choices and the cellars offer a fine choice of wines. The Park Hotel provides programs for the Christmas and New Year holidays. Kenmare is about a three-hour drive from Shannon, a perfect spot for touring the Ring of Kerry.

PARK HOTEL
Owner: Francis Brennan
Kenmare
Co Kerry
tel: (064) 41200
50 bedrooms with private bathrooms
From £76 single to £160 double
Open: April to Christmas
Credit cards: all major
U.S. Rep: Robert Reid
Rep tel: 800-223-6510
Country house

The Cahernane Hotel, built in 1877, was once the grand home of the Herbert family who were the Earls of Pembroke. As a result of their lavish lifestyle the Herberts went into bankruptcy and it is only in recent years that the house has been restored and renovated to its former glory. Pine and blond oak woodwork, over the years worn to a lovely patina, gives a warm feeling to the elegant old house. A blazing log fire and deep sofas in the spacious entrance hall beckon a country house welcome. Up the grand staircase are several comfortable old-fashioned bedrooms offering superb views of the surrounding estate through their tall windows. As a direct contrast to this mellow scene, a wing of modern bedrooms has been added to one side of the house, bridged by a large glass sun-lounge. Here the bright white rooms are tastefully contrasted with vibrant purple, blue and mauve curtains and drapes. The bathrooms are spacious, deluxe modern affairs with luxurious black and brass fitings. In spite of being a large establishment by this guide's standards the Cahernane Hotel manages to keep an intimate country house atmosphere. At Christmas time the hotel offers a traditional yuletide program. Cahernane Hotel is 1 mile from the centre of Killarney on the N71, Kenmare road.

CAHERNANE HOTEL
Manager: Conor O'Connell
Killarney
Co Kerry
tel: (064) 31895
52 bedrooms with private bathrooms
From £43 single to £95 double
Open: Easter to October and Christmas
Credit cards: all major
U.S. Rep: R.S.I.
Rep tel: 800-223-1588
Country house

Carriglea House is an immaculate farmhouse with a breathtaking location overlooking the Lower Killarney Lake and the distant Torc and Mangerton Mountains, and adjacent to Muckross House and Killarney National Park. The rooms are well furnished and lots of well-placed family antiques add a great deal of charm. Five bedrooms are in the main house and four, even lovelier rooms, in an adjacent cottage. Marie Beazley is happy to cook dinner for her guests (all the fruits and vegetables come from the garden) or give them information on where to eat in town. The advantage of staying here is that you can appreciate the extraordinary beauties that surround Killarney without getting involved in the congestion of the town. Carriglea House is 2 miles from the centre of Killarney on the road to Kenmare, the N71. To avoid disappointment advance reservations are recommended.

CARRIGLEA HOUSE
Owners: Michael & Marie Beazley
Muckross Road
Killarney
Co Kerry
tel: (064) 31116
9 bedrooms, 6 with private bathrooms
From £11 to £12.50 per person B & B
Open: Easter to October
Credit cards: none
Farmhouse

Kathleen's Country House has the advantages of being purpose built as a guesthouse and having Kathleen as its effervescent proprietor. She is a person of boundless energy, taking great pride in keeping her house immaculate, cooking scrumptious meals and being a wife and mother. Her two delightful young daughters, Marie and Marguerite, are as friendly and energetic as their mother. The bedrooms are in apple-pie order with tea and coffee makings on hand and color television. The beds are orthopedic, ensuring that guests have a comfortable night's rest. A bright upstairs sun-lounge overlooks the large garden. Kathleen offers a home-cooked set dinner with choices for each course and either red or white house wines. Kathleen's Country House is situated 2 miles from Killarney on the N22, Tralee road, close enough to make it a perfect touring base yet far enough from the hustle and bustle for you to enjoy the peace and quiet of the countryside. To avoid disappointment advance reservations are recommended.

KATHLEEN'S COUNTRY HOUSE
Owner: Kathleen O'Regan-Sheppard
Tralee Road
Killarney
Co Kerry
tel: (064) 32810
11 bedrooms with private bathrooms
From £25 single to £35 double
Open: March to October and Christmas
Credit cards: none
Country guesthouse

Bill and Bobbe Gilmore did not feel that retirement in their native America was for them, so they came to Kinsale and converted Ardcarrig into the lovely country house they had always dreamed of owning. And they run their small establishment just as a country house should be, with every attention given to the care and well-being of their guests. Sherry, port and brandy are on the library table for guests to serve themselves, bathrooms are stocked with "goodies", breakfast is served with the morning paper - the list could run on and on. The layout of the house and grounds makes it unsuitable for children but perfect for those in search of a romantic hideaway - there is even a large outdoor pool (unheated) where you can bask on sunny days. The large green bedroom has stunning views across the rooftops to the harbour below, the pink room is romantic with a flowery print and an impressive four-poster, while the blue room offers woodland views and has its bathroom down the hall. Breakfast is a grand gourmet feast with such delights as cream cheese and dill omelette with smoked salmon making regular appearances. Kinsale has a vast array of restaurants offering every conceivable variety of dinner fare in all price ranges. Ardcarrig is on Compass Hill overlooking Kinsale Harbour directly above the Trident Hotel.

ARDCARRIG
Owners: Bill & Bobbe Gilmore
Compass Hill
Kinsale
Co Cork
tel: (021) 772217
3 bedrooms with private bathrooms
From £27 single to £44 double
Open: April to December
Credit cards: none
Country house

Kinsale is full of historic interest, a town of narrow streets with slate-hung houses surrounding a picturesque harbour.   For a small town Kinsale boasts a remarkable number of gourmet restaurants and you can do no better than to stay at one of them, the Blue Haven.   Sitting at a crossroads in the centre of the town, this pretty white building with blue awnings and trim has tremendous character.   The bar bustles with activity, a sunny conservatory overlooking the flower-filled, walled patio offers excellent bar food and a most reasonably priced tourist menu.   The dining room serves splendid dinners accompanied by fine wine from a list with over 70 selections.   Every bedroom is decorated in soft colors with well-chosen fabrics and thick sand colored carpets.   Several of the larger rooms have sitting areas - all have immaculate modern bathrooms.   Bath towels are artistically arranged atop the beds, each arrangement topped by a fresh summer flower - the same kind of care and attention to detail is found in everything associated with this small hotel run with great style by Brian and Anne Cronin.   The Blue Haven is in the centre of Kinsale - 18 miles south of Cork.

BLUE HAVEN HOTEL
Owners: Brian & Anne Cronin
Kinsale
Co Cork
tel: (021) 772209
9 bedrooms, 7 with private bathrooms
From £30 single to £50 double
Open: March to December
Credit cards: all major
Small hotel

Glebe House is located deep in the countryside, a 15-minute drive from Kinsale. Guy and Kathy are American and Glebe House and Ireland are their home. A house party atmosphere prevails and they do everything themselves from gardening to cleaning and cooking, yet they always have time to sit down for a sherry and a chat with their guests and help them plan their sightseeing adventures. The cooking really merits a special mention, for besides splendid dinners Kathy offers enough creative breakfast menus that you can stay for a week and never have the same thing twice. Belgian waffles heaped high with fresh garden fruits and thick cream, herbed scrambled eggs with kippers and sausage, French toast with homemade preserves - all beautifully presented. The upstairs bedroom is large and has a huge bathroom. The three smaller downstairs bedrooms share a bathroom. To find Glebe House take the N71 from Cork through Innishannon, turn left after the bridge and Glebe House is the first house on the right before entering the village of Ballinadee.

GLEBE HOUSE
Owners: Guy & Kathy Velardi
Ballinadee, Bandon
near Kinsale
Co Cork
tel: (021) 778294
4 bedrooms, 1 with private bathroom
From £12 to £15 per person B & B
Open: May to November
Credit cards: none
Country house

The Lighthouse is my very favorite type of bed & breakfast: tiny snug rooms in an adorable little house on a quiet street, yet within easy strolling distance to everything that a picturesque town has to offer. Art and Ruthann are American-born Irish who returned to Ireland after their children were grown to make Kinsale their home. They bought a small, almost derelict, house and over a period of years added to and restored its small rooms, placing antiques and country-style treasures in every nook and cranny. The finishing touch was a captain's walk atop the house, which offers stunning views across rooftops to Kinsale Harbour. I questioned Ruthann about the advisability of children in a house that is brimming with valuable antique toys - "Absolutely no problem, I love children, I let them admire our things and promptly supply them with dolls and animals, games and toys." I saw evidence of this as I visited the rooms - two beds were piled with stuffed toys on the pillows and games stacked by the side for the little girls who were staying there with their parents. Kinsale is 18 miles south of Cork - stop by The Blue Haven for a map directing you to The Lighthouse.

THE LIGHTHOUSE
Owners: Art & Ruthann Moran-Salinger
The Rock
Kinsale
Co Cork
tel: (201) 772734
6 bedrooms, 3 with private bathrooms
From £10 to £12 per person B & B
Open: February to November
Credit cards: none
Cottage

Nancy Fitzgerald has been the chairwoman of the Irish Farm Holidays Association since its inception over 20 years ago.   She advocates a stay in a farmhouse as being more than a holiday: "It is a feeling of belonging and sharing the traditions of Irish home life with the families who have for generations farmed the land of Ireland." Visitors to Irish farmhouses write to tell her of their experiences: she treasures their compliments and acts upon their complaints.   As if this isn't a full time job in itself, she finds time to make her own guests' stay a memorable one, cooking for them and talking to them in her lovely lounge with its high, ornate plasterwork ceiling and inviting grouping of sofas and chairs round a blazing fire.   This Georgian farmhouse was built by her husband, Norman's, ancestors who were landed gentry hereabouts.   In the early 1930s the estate was divided and Norman now farms the remaining 100 acres.   Upstairs the large airy bedrooms offer a comfortable night's repose and beautiful views through large windows to the surrounding countryside.   There is no central heating but plug-in heaters keep guests warm and snug at night.   The main bathroom with its ball and claw bathtub sitting centre stage is a sight to behold.   Nancy is justly proud that some guests have returned as many as 17 times.   Ashton Grove is signposted on the N8, 8 miles from Cork City.   From Dublin the sign is 4 miles south of Watergrass Hill.

ASHTON GROVE
Owner: Nancy Fitzgerald
Knockraha
Co Cork
tel: (021) 821537
4 bedrooms sharing 2 bathrooms
£9.75 per person B & B
Open: April to October
Credit cards: none
Farmhouse

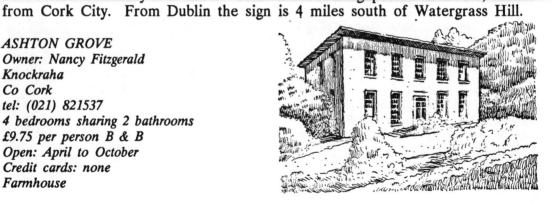

Ceol Na Mara is a simple cottage overlooking Ireland's only fjord, Killary Harbour - a sheltered inlet where oysters are grown in special floating cages.   This is one of the most simple listings in this guide - a picturesque little farmhouse offering panoramic views of the harbour, a quiet and utterly peaceful spot quite literally miles from anywhere - yet perfectly positioned to take driving trips throughout Connemara.   Your arrival will doubtless be announced by loud hee-haws from Lawny, Maura's donkey, a friendly little fellow who trots down to the house to be petted by visitors.   Maura prepares a pot of tea and raisin cake as a welcome for her guests.   Upstairs there are three very simple, plain, little bedrooms set under the sloping eaves of the roof that share a bathroom.   Information on drives through Connemara are provided in each bedroom.   Maura prides herself on her enormous breakfasts of sausage, bacon, black pudding, tomato and egg and is happy to provide a very inexpensive evening meal if requested in advance.   Meals are served in the small sitting cum dining room.   Leenane is between Clifden and Westport on the N59.   From the village of Leenane, turn left onto the Clifden road, skirting the inlet.   Ceol Na Mara is the last house in the village.

CEOL NA MARA
Owner: Maura Kerrigan
Leenane
Connemara
Co Galway
tel: (095) 42249
3 bedrooms sharing 1 bathroom
£9 per person B & B
Open: May to September
Credit cards: none
Farmhouse

Rosleague Manor is an Irish hotel I am extremely fond of - a comfortable country house hotel, overlooking Ballinakill Bay, where the food is enjoyable and the surrounding scenery beautiful.   Connemara is a quiet, sparsely populated land of steep hills, tranquil lakes and grazing sheep, where narrow country lanes lead to little hamlets.   Patrick Foyle, who owns the hotel with his sister Anne, when not occupied in the kitchen, is much in evidence adding his Irish wit to the general camaraderie.   The five course dinner is from a fixed price menu with four or five choices for each course.   Dishes vary with the seasons and include a wide selection of locally caught fish and Connemara lamb.   The hotel is beautifully furnished with lovely old furniture; the lounges cozy with their turf fires and comfortable chairs. After dinner the pub-style bar is a lively place to gather.   While the decor in all the bedrooms is most attractive, the five larger bedrooms in the old house, particularly those with bay views, have more charm than those in the new.   In addition the stables have been converted into holiday cottages.   This is a peaceful place to hide away and a perfect base for exploring Connemara.   Take the N59 from Galway to Clifden, turn right at the church for the 6-mile drive to Rosleague Manor.

ROSLEAGUE MANOR
Owners: Patrick & Anne Foyle
Letterfrack, Connemara
Co Galway
tel: (095) 40101/2
15 bedrooms with private bathrooms
From £30 single to £65 double
Open: Easter to October
Credit cards: all major
U.S. Rep: Robert Reid
Rep tel: 800-223-6510
Country house

If you are seeking a romantic interlude on a gracious country estate you can do no better than to choose Longueville House. Set on a hill overlooking the River Blackwater, this elegant country house offers you the very best of Irish hospitality. The size of the building takes your breath away. It was built by one of Michael O'Callaghan's ancestors in the 1790s - spurred on to grander things by the large sum of money he received for supporting the British Act of Union. In 1866 a lacy wrought iron and glass conservatory was added - filled with baskets of bright summer flowers and palm trees, it is a glorious place to dine. The adjacent Presidents' Restaurant where portraits of former Irish Presidents gaze down benevolently offers the very finest of Irish cuisine. Almost everything that appears on your plate is homemade or grown on the surrounding estate - a bottle of wine from Michael's extensive wine list is a delightful accompaniment to your meal. Bedrooms vary in size from enormous to large - all are beautifully decorated and have modern bathrooms. Guest privileges include 3 miles of salmon and trout fishing on the River Blackwater and free golf at the nearby golf course. The hotel is located on the N72, about a mile west of Mallow and 20 miles north of Cork.

LONGUEVILLE HOUSE
Owners: Michael & Jane O'Callaghan
Mallow
Co Cork
tel: (022) 47156
18 bedrooms with private bathrooms
From £30 single to £80 double
Open: mid-March to mid-December
Credit cards: all major
U.S. Rep: Robert Reid
Rep tel: 800-223-6510
Country house

The hill behind Coolatore House is at the very centre of Ireland: from its top you can see six counties - as far as the Wicklow Mountains (all I saw was blustery rain but despite inclement weather it was fun to stand in the middle of Ireland).   Ann Galvin chatted to me as I sampled the cheesecake she had prepared for the evening meal.   As we visited her six children came repeatedly in and out and I wondered how she could happily hold a conversation, cook dinner and deal with her family all at the same time.   Needless to say, children are very welcome and babysitters readily available.   The farmhouse is spotless and a cheery fire always burns in the drawing room grate.   Up the grand staircase are five nicely decorated bedrooms, two with private bathrooms, the other three sharing two bathrooms.   The Clonmacnois monastic ruins and round tower overlooking the River Shannon are a half hour's drive away and should not be missed.   Coolatore House is midway between Dublin and Galway (N6), 4 miles off the N6, between Horseleap and Moate - the house is very well signposted.

COOLATORE HOUSE
Owner: Ann Galvin
Rosemount
Moate
Co Westmeath
tel: (0902) 36102
5 bedrooms, 2 with private bathrooms
£10 per person B & B
Open: May to September
Credit cards: none
Farmhouse

Roundwood House is situated near Mountrath, in a scenic spot at the foot of the Slieve Bloom Mountains. The house was built in the 1740s for Anthony Sharp upon his return from America - he attached this elegant Palladian home to his grandfather's simple Quaker cottage which still remains at the back of the house. Roundwood House had pretty much fallen into disrepair by the time it was purchased by the Georgian Society in the 1970s - their careful restoration is being continued by Frank and Rosemarie Kennan who forsook the corporate life of IBM. The gray appearance of the outside of the house belies its colorful interior - bright white and blue for the hall and bold yellows, blues and reds for the bedrooms - all done in true Georgian style to give a dramatic impact to the lovely high-ceilinged rooms. Modern bathrooms and central heating are the only visible 20th-century modifications. Collections of books and paintings and beautiful antique furniture combine with the friendliness of your hosts Frank and Rosemarie to make this a most inviting place to stay. There is no need to worry about bringing children along because a portion of the top floor of the house is a nursery with plenty of toys and games to keep children amused for hours. To find Roundwood House take the N7 from Dublin to Mountrath and follow signs for the Slieve Bloom Mountains which will bring you to the house 3 miles out of town.

ROUNDWOOD HOUSE
Owners: Frank & Rosemarie Kennan
Mountrath
Co Laois
tel: (0502) 32120
6 bedrooms with private bathrooms
£16 per person B & B
Closed: January
Credit cards: AX, MC, VS
Country home

Mornington House is a most delightful manor house, offering you a glimpse of what it was like to live the life of the landed gentry of Ireland - at a very reasonable price. Warrick O'Hara is the fifth generation of his family to call this home - and you are encouraged to make it yours.   Family portraits and pictures gaze down upon you as you dine around the enormous dining room table.   Anne has such a reputation for her food that she offers cookery classes locally.   As an accompaniment to your meal you can choose from a red or white house wine.   The two front bedrooms are enormous in size: one has a large brass bed sitting centre stage and requires a climb to get into it.   The other front bedroom has twin brass beds and shares the view across the peaceful grounds.   The third bedroom is small only by comparison with the front rooms, and looks out to the side garden and the woods.   The O'Haras are very involved in foxhunting and while they do not have horses available for guests' use, good horses are available in the area.   Mornington House is a difficult place to find - take the N4 from either Sligo or Dublin to Mullingar, then the Castlepollard road north to Crookedwood where you turn left, then take the first right and the entrance to the house is on your right after a mile.

MORNINGTON HOUSE
Owners: Warrick & Anne O'Hara
Mornington
Multyfarnham near Mullingar
Co Westmeath
tel: (044) 72191
3 bedrooms with private bathrooms
£11 per person B & B
Open: May to September
Credit cards: none
Country house

An air of opulence hangs over Dromoland Castle. Before it became a luxury hotel in 1963 it saw almost 400 years as the ancestral home of the O'Brien clan whose portraits gaze down benignly from the walls. A complete refurbishment of this historic old building was completed in April 1988. Bedrooms and elegant suites in the main house are more stately than the smaller rooms in the adjacent Queen Anne building. An 18-hole golf course and a tennis court are reserved for guests' use and there are plans for an indoor swimming pool. Salmon fishing, horse riding and bird shooting can be arranged nearby. This is a spectacular place to spend either your first or last nights in Ireland if you are flying in or out of Shannon Airport which lies 8 miles to the south.

DROMOLAND CASTLE
Manager: David Pantin
Newmarket-on-Fergus
Co Clare
tel: (061) 71144 telex: 26854
75 bedrooms with private bathrooms
From £120 single to £185 double
Open: March to November
Credit cards: all major
U.S. Rep: Ashford Castle
Rep tel: 800-346-7007
Castle hotel

The old Virginia creeper-covered mansion set amidst gardens overlooking the Newport River presents a welcoming picture to visitors to Newport House.   I soon learned that the pursuit of fish is the main reason for staying here since Newport House has the exclusive fishing rights to the adjacent Newport River and Lough Betra West.   Each morning avid anglers set forth carrying rods and old fashioned straw picnic baskets.   They meet their ghillies at the lake, fish and picnic on one of the lough's islands and return in the evening to proudly display their catch of sea trout and salmon on the hall settle.   Guests then exchange fishy tales over dinner and in the bar - a perfect end to an angler's day!   The public rooms are beautifully decorated,   the bedrooms large and spacious.   Of particular note are the magnificent sweeping central staircase and gallery where sunlight cascades through the rooftop dome and the two suites which boast enormous four-poster beds.   First class food is an important feature of the house: fish is always included on the menu and divine home-smoked salmon is something that Newport House is noted for. An extensive wine list complements the fine cuisine.   This elegant country house reposes between Achill Island and the mountains of Mayo, on the N59 in Newport.

NEWPORT HOUSE
Owners: Kieran & Thelma Thompson
Newport
Co Mayo
tel. (098) 41222 telex: 53740
19 bedrooms with private bathrooms
From £35 single to £65 double
Open: March 20 to September
Credit cards: all major
U.S. Rep: Robert Reid
Rep tel: 800-223-6510
Country house

Thomas and Una Phelan, tired of the busy hustle and bustle of Dublin life, spent a year looking for a quiet country house suitable for conversion into a country inn. Their diligence was rewarded when they found Creacon Lodge: with its mullioned windows and beautiful gardens, they realized it was just the place they had been looking for. Their restoration and refurbishment efforts are now complete and their home stands in tiptop condition. The lounge is full of comfy chairs and sofas, making it the perfect spot for guests to gather for before- and after-dinner drinks and a chat. Una prides herself on her lovely food and both she and Thomas do a very gracious job serving it to their guests. The small bedrooms are tucked under the roof of the house and their tiny windows offer views of the garden. Three bedrooms have bathrooms en suite with showers while the remaining two share a bathroom. John F. Kennedy's ancestors came from these parts and Creacon Lodge is the perfect spot to stay and visit the nearby park that has been created in his memory. It is only a 25-mile drive from Rosslare Harbour, making it ideal for your first nights in Ireland if you are arriving by ferry from Wales or France. Take the N25 from Waterford to the outskirts of New Ross where you follow signs for the John F. Kennedy Memorial Park. You will find Creacon Lodge midway between the main road and the park on the left-hand side of the road.

CREACON LODGE
Owners: Thomas and Una Phelan
New Ross
Co Wexford
tel: (051) 21897
5 bedrooms, 3 with private bathrooms
From £14 to £16.50 per person B & B
Open: all year
Credit cards: none
Country home

Guests at Currarevagh House find themselves entering a world reminiscent of that at the turn of the century.   Tranquility reigns supreme and the good old-fashioned way is the way things are done at Currarevagh House.   However, do not be afraid that you will be deprived of central heating and private bathrooms, for this is not the case.   A set dinner is offered promptly at 8pm: a gong announces dinner and while there are no choices, the helpings are of generous proportions.   For breakfast the dishes and an array of tempting food is spread on the sideboard for you to help yourself.   The hotel is happy to pack you a picnic lunch, and as a special treat for those who are returning that night they will pack it in a quaint old tin box bound by a leather strap.   It's all very old-fashioned but I must admit that I thoroughly enjoyed it - the Hodgsons really do manage to create the illusion of being back in Victorian times.   Nearby Lough Corrib, the second largest lake in Ireland, is a haven for fishermen and Harry can arrange for fishing.   Guests return year after year, so it is advisable to make reservations, particularly for the busy summer months.   From Galway take the N59 to Oughterard, turn right in the centre of the village and follow the lakeshore for the 4-mile drive to the house.

CURRAREVAGH HOUSE
Owners: June & Harry Hodgson
Oughterard, Connemara
Co Galway
tel: (091) 82313
16 bedrooms with private bathrooms
From £31.50 single to £63 double
Open: Easter to October
Credit cards: none
U.S. Rep: Robert Reid
Rep tel: 800-223-6510
Country house

Ardeen was an especially welcome haven after exploring the Donegal coast on a particularly gloomy wet summer's day.   This attractive Victorian house was once the town doctor's home and Anne Campbell and her husband, who owns the local hardware store, had always admired Ardeen's airy rooms and large riverside garden, so, when it came up for sale, they jumped at the opportunity to call it home. Breakfast around the large dining room table is the only meal that Anne prepares, though she is happy to offer advice on where to eat in Ramelton.   The bedrooms are decorated to a high standard and guests can plan their sightseeing from the warmth of the sitting room.   Ardeen is an ideal base for exploring the Donegal coastline, visiting Glenveagh National Park and the Glebe Art Gallery with its fine collection of Irish paintings.   If you are arriving from Donegal take the N56 to Letterkenny and on the outskirts of the town look for the T72, signposted for Rathmullen.   Its a 7-mile drive to Ramelton: when you reach the river turn right, following the bank, and Ardeen is on your right.

ARDEEN
Owner: Anne Campbell
Ramelton
Co Donegal
tel: (074) 51243
4 bedrooms sharing 1 bathroom
£10 per person B & B
Open: Easter to September
Credit cards: none
Country home

Rathmullan House has a perfect setting amidst acres of lovingly tended gardens that slope down to a sandy beach with views of the mountains across Lough Swilly. This large, rambling country house is decorated in a plain style with the exception of the ornate pavillion dining room where fabric has been gathered across the ceiling to give a tentlike appearance to the three interconnecting rooms.   A three or four course dinner is offered with enough selections in each course to satisfy the most discerning diner.   After dinner coffee is offered on a help-yourself basis in the coffee lounge.   The very nicest bedrooms face the lough and are furnished in a traditional style.   The remaining bedrooms are a mixed bunch - some have co-ordinating country-style drapes and bedspreads while others have a mismatched contemporary look to them.   Downstairs is a convivial cellar bar.   Rathmullan House is ideally situated for visiting the rugged Donegal coastline, Glenveagh National Park and the Glebe Art Gallery.   From Donegal take the N15 to Ballybofey, the N56 to the outskirts of Letterkenny, through Ramelton, and follow the shores of Lough Swilly through Rathmullan.   The house is on your right as you leave the village.

RATHMULLAN HOUSE
Owners: Bob & Robin Wheeler
Rathmullan near Letterkenny
Co Donegal
tel: (074) 58188
19 bedrooms, 14 with private bathrooms
From £30 single to £70.50 double
Open: Easter to mid-October
Credit cards: all major
U.S. Rep: Robert Reid
Rep tel: 800-223-6510
Country house

"There is nothing which has yet been contrived by man by which so much happiness is produced as by a good inn" - the staff of Hunter's Hotel has adopted Samuel Johnson's words as a creed and it certainly describes them. The hotel retains much of its original 18th-century charm, with creaking wooden floorboards, polished tile floors, old prints, beams and antique furniture. Tom and Patrick Gelletlie are the fifth generation of their family to operate this inn, assisting their mother Maureen. Two fine traditions endure at Hunter's: old-fashioned Sunday lunches and afternoon teas of oven-fresh scones and strawberry jam. All the bedrooms are prettily decorated. Room 17, a twin-bedded ground floor room with a private garden entrance, stands out as a particular favorite. Inexpensive bedrooms without private bathrooms share rather utilitarian bathroom facilities. A flower-filled garden stretches along the side of the hotel and down to the River Vartry - it's a perfect spot to sit on a warm summer evening and as you soak in the beauty of the garden it is hard to realize that you are only 28 miles south of Dublin. To find this idyllic spot, take the N11 south from Dublin to Ashford and Hunter's Hotel is signposted 1 mile down a country lane to your left as you enter the village.

HUNTER'S HOTEL
Owner: Maureen Gelletlie
Rathnew
Co Wicklow
tel: (0404) 4106
17 bedrooms, 10 with private bathrooms
From £27 single to £55 double
Open: all year
Credit cards: all major
U.S. Rep: Robert Reid
Rep tel: 800-223-6510
Old coaching inn

Tinakilly House maintains the purpose for which it was designed - gracious living. The house was built in the 1870s by Captain Robert Halpin, the commander of the ship Great Eastern which laid the first telegraph cable connecting Europe to America.   Tinakilly House's ornate staircase is reputed to be a copy of the one on this ship.   Whether or not this is true is a matter of conjecture, but the captain certainly spared no expense when he built this classical house with its fine pitch pine doors and shutters and ornate plasterwork ceilings.   William and Bee Powers bought the house as a family home but found the cost of restoration and its size too large, so decided to open it as a hotel.   They have done a splendid job, furnishing the house with appropriate Victorian furniture and adding a welcoming charm to the place.   Second-floor bedrooms are expansive in size, while those on the third floor, tucked into the original attics, are snug and country-cozy and proportionately less expensive.   William and Bee encourage their guests to use Tinakilly House as a countryside base for exploring Dublin, Glendalough and the Wicklow Mountains. From Dublin take the N11 (Wexford road) to Rathnew village.   Turn left, towards Wicklow, and the entrance to the hotel is on your left as you leave the village.

TINAKILLY HOUSE
Owners: William & Bee Powers
Rathnew
Co Wicklow
tel: (0404) 69274/67227
14 bedrooms with private bathrooms
From £54 single to £97 double
Closed: Christmas to February
Credit cards: AX, VS
U.S. Rep: Robert Reid
Rep tel: 800-223-6510
Country house

Coopershill is a grand Georgian farmhouse set amongst 500 acres of grounds. Brian and Lindy returned to their home in 1986 to continue the tradition of welcoming guests to this fine country house that has been home to the O'Hara family since 1774 when the house was built. Much of the grand antique furniture is as old as the house itself. All but one of the bedrooms have the original four-poster or half tester beds, but of course with modern spring mattresses, and toasty electric blankets. All the bedrooms are large and have private bathrooms, though two are across the hall. Ancestors' portraits gaze down upon you in the dining room and the set dinner is served from family silverware on the enormous sideboard. The public rooms and hallways are of vast proportions. Fires and central heating warm downstairs while upstairs each bedroom has a powerful fan heater to keep the chill away. From Dublin take the N4 to Drumfin (11 miles south of Sligo). Turn right towards Riverstown and Coopershill is on your right 2 miles before you come to the village.

COOPERSHILL FARMHOUSE
Owners: Brian & Lindy O'Hara
Riverstown
Co Sligo
tel: (071) 65108 telex: 40301
6 bedrooms with private bathrooms
£25 per person B & B
Open: mid-March to October
Credit cards: AX, MC, VS
U.S. Rep: Robert Reid
Rep tel: 800-223-6510
Country house

Ballymaloe House is a rambling 17th-century manor house built on to an old Norman keep surrounded by lawns, a 9-hole golf course kept cropped by grazing sheep and 400 acres of farmland. Myrtle Allen's personal touch, however, makes you feel like a guest in her family home, which this has been since 1948. Myrtle has established an international reputation for her cuisine and most ingredients come from their own farms while the fish comes direct from the nearby harbour. Guests gather before dinner in the lounge to make their selections from the set menu which offers four or five choices for each of the courses. The bedrooms in the main house come in all shapes and sizes from large and airy to cozy and panelled. Surrounding a courtyard, the smaller stable bedrooms offer country cottage charm, sprigged flowered wallpaper and beamed ceilings for those on the upper floor. Most unusual accommodations are in the doll-sized gatekeeper's cottage which is just large enough to have a bathroom on the ground floor and a ladder to the twin-bedded room above with its tiny log-burning fireplace. Shanagarry is 20 miles southeast of Cork and signposted from the N25 (Cork to Waterford road).

BALLYMALOE HOUSE
Owner: Myrtle Allen
Shanagarry, Midleton
Co Cork
tel: (021) 652531 telex: 75208
30 bedrooms with private bathrooms
From £52 single to £74 double
Closed for Christmas
Credit cards: all major
U.S. Rep: Robert Reid
Rep tel: 800-223-6510
Country house

Charles and Mary Cooper gained culinary experience in England, France and Switzerland before returning to Ireland to open a restaurant at Knockmuldowney in 1982. Their endeavor has been a great success and the addition of bedrooms in 1986 has enabled them to offer overnight hospitality to those who come to eat. The bedrooms are quite large, nicely decorated, have the odd antique piece here and there and enjoy views of the garden and the Ox Mountains or Ballisadare Bay. The restaurant has a very simple, quite modern decor and offers both a set dinner and a short a la carte menu. Vegetables and fruits are grown in the garden and fish and meat are obtained fresh from the market. There are lots of activities to occupy guests in the area: indoor riding, the beach and golf. The countryside that Yeats wrote about is all around you - he is buried nearby at the churchyard in Drumcliff. Charles and Mary are happy to pick guests up from the Sligo train station 5 miles away. Drivers should take the N4 from Dublin almost to Sligo. In Ballisodare, cross the bridge, go under the railway bridge and turn immediately left towards Strandhill then follow the coast to Knockmuldowney.

KNOCKMULDOWNEY
Owners: Charles & Mary Cooper
Culleenamore
Strandhill near Sligo
Co Sligo
tel: (071) 68122 telex: 40301
6 bedrooms with private bathrooms
From £32 single to £52 double
Open: mid-March to October
Credit cards: all major
U.S. Rep: Robert Reid
Rep tel: 800-223-6510
Country house

Charles Waterhouse spent several years of the Second World War around the Khyber Pass pursuing a colorful career as the aide-de-camp to the Governor of the Northwest Territories of India.   Subsequently he settled at Tahilla Cove and built this delightful resort overlooking a most picturesque bay.   The furnishings and decor throughout are very plain, the atmosphere most inviting and the company of your hosts, fellow guests and the locals just what you come to Ireland to experience. In the evening guests gather with locals in the bar to chat with Charles and Molly, while son Jamie tends the bar.   Dinner and breakfast are served in the dining room whose large windows frame a magnificent view of the cove and its little harbour. The bedrooms share the same bucolic view: four are in the main house and an additional five across the garden in a separate building.   The bedrooms are plainly furnished and have a pleasant old-fashioned air to them. An especially memorable daytrip can be arranged to Skellig Michael, a small rocky island topped by an ancient monastery reached by climbing hundreds of winding stairs from the landing cove - Jamie can make your reservation and supply you with a packed lunch. Tahilla lies 11 miles west of Kenmare on the Ring of Kerry.

TAHILLA COVE GUESTHOUSE
Owner: The Waterhouse Family
Tahilla
Ring of Kerry
Co Kerry
tel: (064) 45104
9 bedrooms with private bathrooms
£18 per person B & B
Open: Easter to October
Credit cards: all major
Seaside guesthouse

Fanad Head is a lovely peninsula jutting out into the Atlantic Ocean at the far north of Ireland.   If you are looking for a place to stay that has that end-of-the-earth feel about it, a place where you will see few visitors and be surrounded by beautiful countryside, then you can do no better than to stay with Sadie Sweeney at her farmhouse.   This 100-year-old creeper-covered house, its windowboxes laden with colorful flowers, presents a welcoming picture to visitors - the interior does not disappoint for Sadie has taken great care to decorate the bedrooms prettily with matching curtains and wallpaper.   Three are roomy doubles and twins and two are cozy singles. All five share two nicely appointed bathrooms. Wholesome farmhouse food is served in the dining room - the meats and vegetables fresh from the farm.   Guests are welcome to visit the farmyard and watch, or participate in, the cow milking.   From Letterkenny take the R245 through Ramelton and follow signs for Kerrykeel where you turn sharp left in the centre of the village and follow the ocean to the tiny village of Rosnakill.   The farmhouse is on your left just as you enter Tamney.

SWEENEY'S FARMHOUSE
Owner: Sadie Sweeney
Tamney near Kerrykeel
Fanad Head
Co Donegal
tel: (074) 59011
5 bedrooms sharing 2 bathrooms
£9.50 per person B & B
Open: April to September
Credit cards: none
Farmhouse

In 1800 the Countess of Belvedere built a crescent of homes around a village green creating the village of Tyrellspass. The homes have since passed into private hands and, fortunately for visitors, what was the rent collector's house has been converted into a charming village inn. Gay windowboxes and tubs of flowers decorate the outside and tables and chairs proffer a place to sit with a pint and watch the world go by. Accommodation is offered in cottage-style bedrooms, each nicely furnished with Rossmore furniture and decorated with matching flowery drapes and spreads. Casual meals and an extensive selection of barfood is offered from a hot and cold buffet in the bar. More formal dining is in order in the large dining room where the tables are attractively set with pink and white linens coordinating with the decor (plastic chairs are a jarring feature). Tyrrellspass lies 50 miles from Dublin on the main Dublin to Galway road (N6).

VILLAGE HOTEL
Owners: Peter & Brenda Pierson
Tyrrellspass
Co Meath
tel: (044) 23171
10 bedrooms with private bathrooms
£20 per person B & B
Open: all year
Credit cards: all major
U.S. Rep: Jane Condon
Rep tel: 212-986-4373
Country inn

This working farm with 100 acres laid down to grain production and cattle is a delight for adults and children alike: as well as farm activities there are pony rides (on a leading rein), tennis courts and a childrens' game room.   Whenever David Kent is not occupied with farm matters, he loves to talk to visitors and discuss the farm and what to do and see in the area.   (The Waterford crystal factory is a big draw and Margaret is happy to make an appointment to tour.)   Margaret is one of those people who shows her appreciation of her guests by feeding them lavishly. She delights in the preparation of dishes made from beef from the farm homegrown fruits (strawberries, raspberries, gooseberries, apples and rhubarb, to name but a few) and vegetables - her specialty is her homemade ice cream.   Guests are served after-dinner coffee in the lounge and often linger for discussions around the fireside.   Upstairs several of the simply decorated bedrooms are large enough to accommodate an extra child or children.   To find the house take the road from Waterford toward Dunmore East.   After about 4 miles, at the Maxol garage, take the left fork toward Passage East.   Foxmount Farm is signposted on the right about 2 miles before Passage East.

FOXMOUNT FARM
Owner: Margaret Kent
Dunmore East Road
Waterford
Co Waterford
tel: (051) 74308
6 bedrooms sharing 2 bathrooms
£10 per person B & B
Open: April to mid October
Credit cards: none
Farmhouse

The Old Coach House is a favorite because the house is especially lovely and because Liz and Michael Purnell make you feel at home.   The Purnells have a very caring, casual fuss-free manner that makes a stay here particularly pleasant.   The Old Coach House was once a huge barn on the grounds of their home.   Michael's conversion has been done with great style: lattice windows have been inset in the thick walls and the rooms have been designed to give a spacious, country-cozy feel. The large sitting room is the centre of the house where guests gather to relax and chat.   In the dining room the well polished table is laid with china, glass and silver. Liz enjoys cooking a wide repertoire of dishes. Above, the bedrooms are particularly spacious and beautifully furnished: smart Sanderson wallpapers grace the walls and match the drapes and bedspreads.   This is a perfect place to stay to enjoy a visit to the nearby Waterford crystal factory and the John F. Kennedy Memorial Park. From Waterford turn toward Dunmore East (by the Tower Hotel). After about 4 miles (at the Maxol garage) take the left fork toward Passage East, take the first left, past the modern houses and The Old Coach House is on your right.

THE OLD COACH HOUSE
Owners: Michael & Liz Purnell
Blenheim Heights
Waterford
Co Waterford
tel: (051) 74471
4 bedrooms with private bathrooms
£15 per person B & B
Closed for Christmas
Credit cards: none
Country home

Westport is one of the few architecturally pre-designed towns in Ireland. Its architect, James Wyatt, made the most of the site: the river is walled in and treelined, and he designed an attractive octagonal town centre. The waterfront lies away from the town, many of its old buildings transformed into pubs and restaurants. Just a short drive beyond the waterfront lies Rosbeg House with Clew Bay dotted with little green islands at its front and Croagh Patrick (the cone shaped holy mountain of Ireland) at its rear. Brian and Kay O'Brien came here several years ago and have turned this 250-year-old house into a comfortable place to stay. The two larger front bedrooms have private bathrooms and four smaller bedrooms share two bathrooms. A television room is there for guests to use and breakfast is taken in an attractively decorated room just off the large family kitchen. Brian and Kay recommend places nearby for dinner. Westport is 65 miles northwest of Galway. Rosbeg House is 2 miles to the west of the town on the road to Croagh Patrick.

ROSBEG HOUSE
Owners: Brian & Kay O'Brien
Westport
Co Mayo
tel: (098) 25879
6 bedrooms, 2 with private bathrooms
From £11 to £14 per person B & B
Open: March to October
Credit cards: none
Farmhouse

If you are arriving in (or leaving) Ireland by ferry from Rosslare Harbour Clonard House is a convenient and most enjoyable place to spend the night. Kathleen Hayes won the 1986 "Farmhouse of the Year" competition which is judged on the quality of the accommodation, the high standard of food and the warmth of welcome offered to visitors. Building on the house began in 1783 and the owner planned to build himself a grand three-story structure but skirmishes with the British continually interrupted construction and depleted funds so he got no farther than the second floor, leaving the grand central staircase to curve into the ceiling. The bedrooms all have bathrooms en suite and are simply decorated in pastel shades. The five front bedrooms are smaller and offer lovely views across farmland to the distant sea. The four course dinner offers a choice between salmon and steak but for guests who are staying longer than an overnight Kathleen varies the menu. If you are arriving from the ferry the house is signposted on the Rosslare-Wexford ring road. If you are arriving from Wexford take the Duncannon road (by the Talbot Hotel) out of town for about 2 miles to the roundabout on the ring road where you see a sign for Clonard House.

CLONARD HOUSE
Owner: Kathleen Hayes
Clonard Great
Wexford
Co Wexford
tel: (053) 23141
8 bedrooms with private bathrooms
£11 per person B & B
Open: May to November
Credit cards: none
Farmhouse

When Otto and Patricia built their home they used a traditional Georgian design and gave it an old-fashioned feel with ceiling moldings and traditional doors and decor. Friends suggested they open as a farm guesthouse so, taking the plunge, they added extra bathrooms and opened their doors. How fortunate they did, for now visitors to the Wicklow area can enjoy this welcoming home and the flower-filled garden that surrounds it. Patricia, who loves to cook, prepares good homely meals, with homemade soup, wiener schnitzel accompanied by farm fresh vegetabes and followed by plum pie being the order of the day for our meal. (Otto came to Ireland from East Germany so Patricia enjoys serving a mixture of Irish and German dishes.) Proportions are large enough to satisfy even the heartiest of eaters. The bedrooms are decorated in soft pastels, the orthopedic beds topped by soft woolen bedspreads. One guestroom has the advantage of a king-size bed and a private bathroom. Wicklow is a pleasant small town round a harbour just an hour's drive south of Dublin and the Dun Laoghaire ferry and north of the Rosslare ferry. The Wicklow Mountains, Powerscourt Gardens, Glendalough and the Vale of Avoca are close at hand. As you enter Wicklow town turn right at the Grand Hotel, towards the top of the hill take the first right on Ashtown Lane and Lissadell House is on your right.

LISSADELL HOUSE
Owners: Otto and Patricia Klaue
Ashtown Lane off Marlton Road
Wicklow
Co Wicklow
tel: (0404) 67458
4 bedrooms, 2 with private bathrooms
£11 to £13 per person B & B
Open: March to November
Farmhouse

Map 1

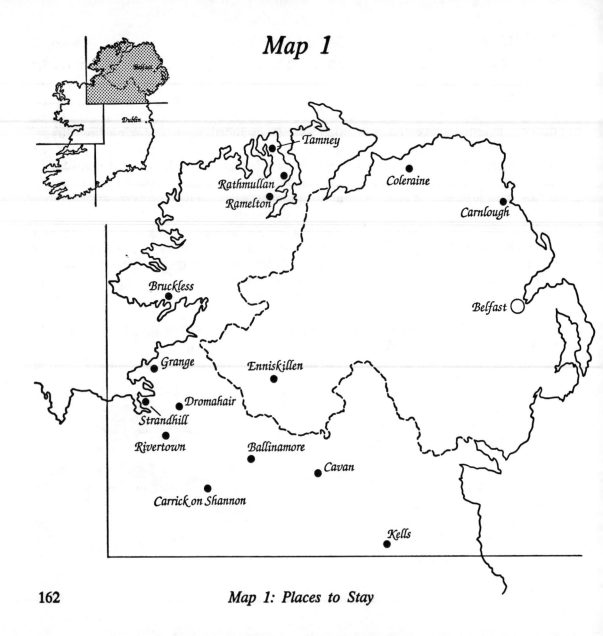

Map 1: Places to Stay

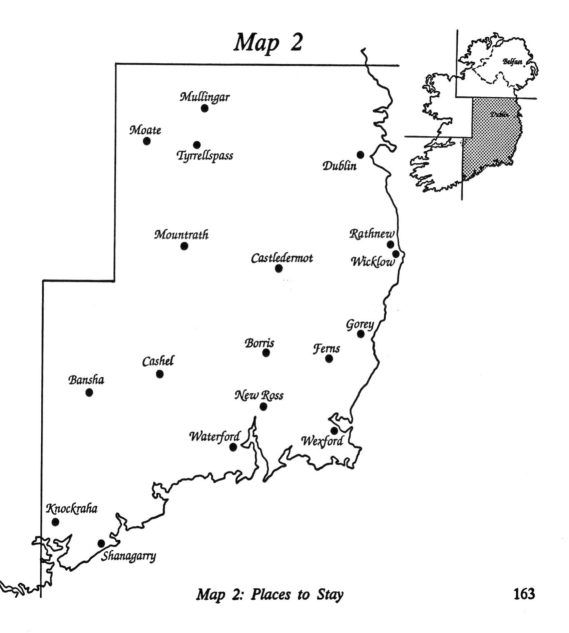

Map 2

Mullingar

Moate

Tyrrellspass

Dublin

Mountrath

Castledermot

Rathnew

Wicklow

Gorey

Borris

Ferns

Cashel

Bansha

New Ross

Waterford

Wexford

Knockraha

Shanagarry

Belfast

Dublin

Map 2: Places to Stay

Map 3

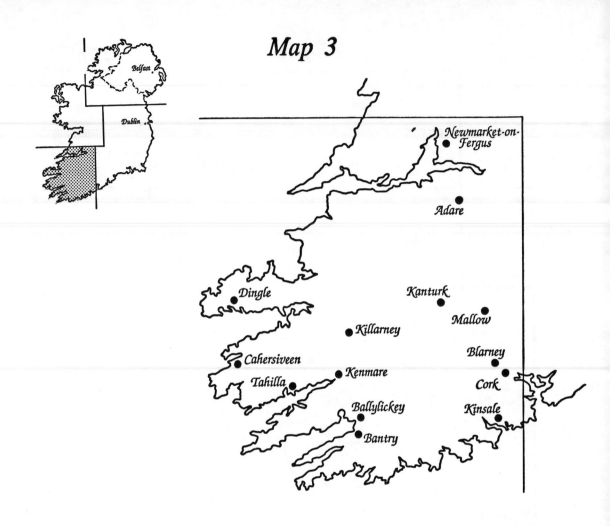

Map 3: Places to Stay

Map 4

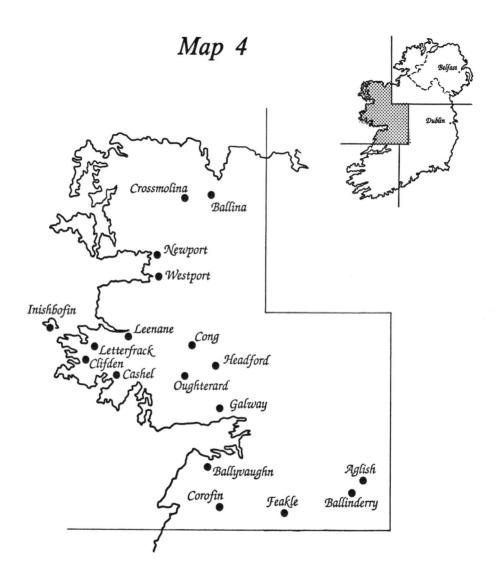

Map 4: Places to Stay

Overview Map
of Driving Itineraries

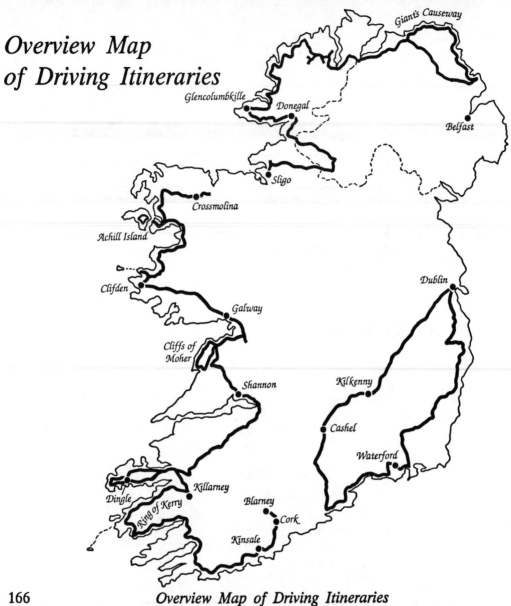

Giant's Causeway

Glencolumbkille   Donegal

Belfast

Sligo

Crossmolina

Achill Island

Clifden

Galway

Dublin

Cliffs of
Moher

Shannon

Kilkenny

Cashel

Waterford

Dingle

Killarney

Ring of Kerry

Blarney

Cork

Kinsale

Overview Map of Driving Itineraries

Index

Abbey Villa, Adare, 14, 74
Achill Island, 38
Adare, 14
Adare, Abbey Villa 14, 74
Adare, Dunraven Arms 14, 75
Aghadoe, 20
Aglish, Ballycormac House, 76
Ailwee Caves, 33
Anglesea Townhouse, Dublin, 109
Arbutus Lodge, Cork, 101
Ardcarrig, Kinsale, 26, 132
Ardeen, Ramelton, 48, 147
Ardmore Monastic Site, 62
Ariel House, Dublin, 110
Arthurstown, 60
Ashford Castle, Cong, 100
Ashton Grove, Knockraha, 136
Assolas Country House, Kanturk, 125
Atlantic Drive, 38
Aughnanure Castle, 34
Avoca, 60
Ballina, Mount Falcon, 39, 77
Ballinamore, Riversdale, 78
Ballinderry, Gurthalougha House, 79
Ballinspittle, 25
Ballintoy Harbour, 52
Ballintubber Abbey, 40
Ballycastle, 52
Ballycormac House, Aglish, 76

INN DISCOVERIES FROM OUR READERS

Future editions of *KAREN BROWN'S COUNTRY INN GUIDES TO EUROPE* are going to include a new feature - a list of hotels recommended by our readers. We have received many letters describing wonderful inns you have discovered; however, we have never included them until we had the opportunity to make a personal inspection. This seemed a waste of some marvelous "tips". Therefore, in order to feature them we have decided to add a new section called "Inn Discoveries from Our Readers".

If you have a favorite discovery you would be willing to share with other travellers who love to travel the "inn way", please let us hear from you and include the following information:

1. *Your name, address and telephone number.*

2. *Name, address and telephone number of "your inn".*

3. *Brochure or picture of inn (we cannot return material).*

4. *Written permission to use an edited version of your description.*

5. *Would you want your name, city and state included in the book?*

In addition to our current guide books, we are also researching future books in Europe and updating those previously published. We would appreciate comments on any of your favorites. The types of inns we would love to hear about are those with special "olde-worlde" ambiance, charm and atmosphere. We need a brochure or picture so that we can select those which most closely follow the mood of our guides. We look forward to hearing from you. Thank you.

Karen Brown's Country Inn Guides to Europe

The Most Reliable & Informative Series on European Country Inns

Detailed itineraries guide you through the countryside and suggest a cozy inn for each night's stay. In the hotel section, every listing has been inspected and chosen for its romantic ambiance. Charming accommodations reflect every price range, from budget hideaways to deluxe palaces.

Order Form

KAREN BROWN'S COUNTRY INN GUIDES

Please ask in your local bookstore for **KAREN BROWN'S COUNTRY INN** guides.
If the books you want are unavailable, you may order directly from the publisher.

AUSTRIAN COUNTRY INNS & CASTLES $12.95
CALIFORNIA - COUNTRY INNS & ITINERARIES $12.95 (1989)
ENGLISH, WELSH & SCOTTISH COUNTRY INNS $12.95
EUROPEAN COUNTRY CUISINE - ROMANTIC INNS & RECIPES $10.95
EUROPEAN COUNTRY INNS - BEST ON A BUDGET $14.95
FRANCE - BEST BED & BREAKFASTS $12.95 (1989)
FRENCH COUNTRY INNS & CHATEAUX $12.95
GERMAN COUNTRY INNS & CASTLES $12.95
IRISH COUNTRY INNS $12.95
ITALIAN COUNTRY INNS & VILLAS $12.95
PORTUGUESE COUNTRY INNS & POUSADAS $12.95
SCANDINAVIAN COUNTRY INNS & MANORS $12.95
SPANISH COUNTRY INNS & PARADORS $12.95
SWISS COUNTRY INNS & CHALETS $12.95

Name _____   *Street* _____

City _____   *State* _____ *Zip* _____

Add $2.00 for the first book and .50 for each additional book for postage & packing.
California residents add 6 1/2% sales tax.
Indicate the number of copies of each title. Send in form with your check to:

KAREN BROWN'S COUNTRY INN GUIDES
P.O Box 70
San Mateo, CA 94401
(415) 342-9117

This guide is especially written for the individual traveller who wants to plan his own vacation. However, should you prefer to join a group, Town and Country - Hillsdale Travel can recommend tours using country inns with romantic ambiance for many of the nights' accommodation. Or, should you want to organize your own group (art class, gourmet society, bridge club, church group, etc.) and travel with friends, custom tours can be arranged using small hotels with special charm and appeal. For further information please call:

Town & Country - Hillsdale Travel
16 East Third Avenue
San Mateo, California 94401

(415) 342-5591
Outside California 800-227-6733

KAREN BROWN travelled to France when she was 19 to write *French Country Inns & Chateaux* - the first book of what has grown to be an extremely successful series on European country inns. With 12 guides now on the market, Karen's staff has expanded, but she is still involved in planning, researching, formatting and editing each of the guides in her Country Inn series and returns frequently to Europe to update her guides. Karen, her husband, Rick, and their young children, Alexandra and Richard, live in the San Francisco Bay area.

JUNE BROWN author of *Irish Country Inns* and co-author of *English, Welsh & Scottish Country Inns* and *German Country Inns & Castles* has an extensive background in travel. Born in Sheffield, England, travel has remained one of June's great loves. June lives in the San Francisco Bay area with her husband, Tony, and their son Simon.

BARBARA TAPP is the talented artist responsible for the interior sketches of *Irish Country Inns*. Raised in Australia, Barbara studied in Sydney at the School of Interior Design. Although Barbara continues with freelance projects, she devotes much of her time to illustrating Karen's Country Inn guides. Barbara lives in the San Francisco Bay area with her husband, Richard, and their three children.